Self-Motivation

Published by
Lotus Press Publishers & Distributors

Self- Motivation

John Yager

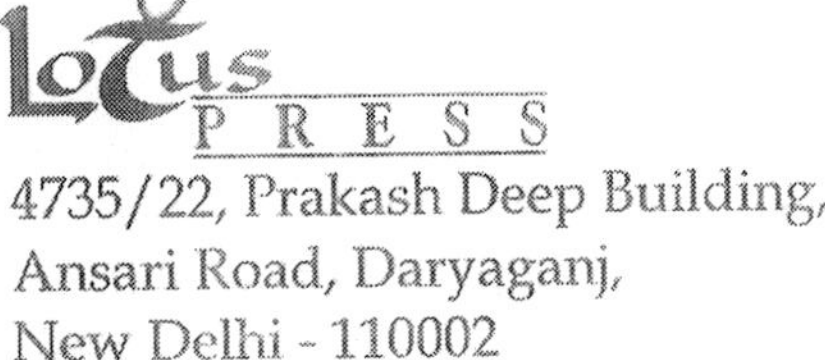

4735/22, Prakash Deep Building,
Ansari Road, Daryaganj,
New Delhi - 110002

Lotus Press : Publishers & Distributors
Unit No. 220, 2nd Floor, 4735/22, Prakash Deep Building,
Ansari Road, Darya Ganj, New Delhi- 110002
Ph. 41325510, 98118-38000
• E-mail : lotuspress1984@gmail.com
www.lotuspress.co.in

Self Motivation

ISBN : 81-8382-028-X

Printed & Published by : **Lotus Press Publishers & Distributors,** New Delhi- 2

Preface

This book has been written with the purpose of sharing what I have learnt from the various sources, books, lectures, experiences and, of course, the biggest teacher and lesson—'The life'. Many books have been written on 'Self -Motivation' but either they are too matter of fact or too religious, philosophical and beyond the comprehension of the readers. I have tried to strike a balance by including bath practical and philosophical viewpoints. Illustrations, pictures, interesting anecdotes have been included to increase the flavour of contents. I truly hope the readers pick up the useful hints given in this book and enjoy the matters discussed.

While writing several sections of this book I felt that I needed a dose of my own medicine. While suggesting several ingredients for success and achievement of goals, I felt that I myself badly needed these ingredients. I have no qualms in confessing that many a time we become aware of what we need only when we suggest things to others. The writing of this book has surely served as an eye opener for me. I take this opportunity to thank the publisher, Mr. A.J. Sehgal, for giving me the opportunity to present this book to the readers.

I will be overjoyed if the readers have anything useful, interesting and inspiring to share with me and others.

I would like to make one point clear: there may be certain contradictios in some sections of this book. 'Flight' may be prescribed somewhere and 'fight' at other places. Nothing can be generalised exceptions, 'Individual' personalities, unique situations all must be given careful consideration and credence before making a *decision.*. The readers are advised to exercise their discretion in all their attempts and endeavours.

Author

Contents

Part-I

INTRODUCTION

1

INTRODUCTION

A hen can supply the necessary heat for an egg to be hatched but the chick has to come out on its own will. Only if the chick has the necessary will, vigour and motivation will it come out. No hen can supply these qualities. This in-built motivation is the most characteristic attribute (and natural too) of a living creature. It is the root cause by which this entire world functions.

Only people who have this motivation, interest, and 'eagerness to acheive' make this world a better place. If we can realise this 'inbuilt strength' which is naturally present in us (a gift from nature), our victory is guaranteed. We will win every challenge, every battle. This winning strategy has been adopted in the various developed countries. India needs this strategy now. Indians, especially the younger generation, have to realise their inbuilt potential; this can be achieved by self-motivation.

This book discusses some aspects of motivation. How one can develop self-confidence and and achieve success (in money, or anything one wants) by using one's inner strengths and potentials?

Unless the parrot has the motivation to fly out and enjoy the freedom, opening the cage will have no effect.

Most of the books written on this subject are usually reproductions of Western books on the same subject. The Indian books reflect and mimic the foreign books. India needs its own concept of motivation. We cannot 'import' confidence and motivation. They are not commodities. India can proudly boast of spiritual leaders like Vivekananda who gave the entire world a lesson on confidence, motivation and inbuilt potentials/strengths–unique and natural–waiting to get unleashed in each individual. The *Bhagavad Gita* speaks only about these. India doesn't need any Western canned food-like motivation lessons. India has rich seeds (full of vigour and strength) of motivation, supplied to it generation after generation by various great leaders and spiritual luminaries, and these seeds can sprout on their own without any external help. One has to just identify the right seed.

The *Bhagavad Gita* is a truly motivating work.

Frost's lines, 'The woods are lovely, dark and deep/But I have and promises to keep/And miles to go before I sleep, are excellent in kindling one's lazy spirits, boosting the morale or motivating one's heart and mind. The following lines.

'तस्मात् सर्वेषु कालेषु मामनुस्मर झध्य च..... of the *Bhagavad Gita* (Chapter VIII) in which Krishna says 'Remember me and fight!' are no less inspring.

The *Bhagavad Gita* is a motivating work, basing its eternal relevance to the problems of human life and its universal approach taught on the battlefield of Kurukshetra urging Arjuna to fight. It has nothing to do with wars or battles of bloodshed, but only with the discharging of ones'sacred duties of life, however unpleasant they may be. The above mentioned lines can help and inspire us beleaguered with serious problems in life. The Hindu tradition compares the *Mahabharata* to a lamp and the *Gita* to the light in it. This light has motivated scores of people in India and abroad.

This book has included both Western and Indian spiritual thought to present a comprehensive picture to motivate and unleash the dormant potential in every individual who reads this book.

****

2
SELF-ESTEEM

To achieve anything in life the first important step is to have self-confidence, self-respect and self-esteem. A person must be able to answer in the affirmative when asked the following questions.

1. Do you like yourself?
2. Can you tolerate yourself?
3. Do you love yourself?
4. Do you dress well? Do you walk well? Can you eat in style?

> → SELF-ESTEEM and SELF-RESPECT are very important in life
> → SELF-EVALUATION must yield a high value.
> → 'Your life is in your hands'. Where there is a will there is a way.

5. Does your name feature in the list of your most respected or admired people? If so, where does it come: in the first place or at the last?

Only when our own name features in the list of our admired/respected individuals will we be able to get respect and admiration from others. First we must be capable of being loved by ourselves, only then can we expect love from others.

On self-evaluation' we must be able to state a high value of our personality, talents, virtues or nature. Self-assessement must yield a good value of ourselves. A person who has self-respect and self-esteem never faces defeat/failure. If we don't have these qualities we must cultivate them. We must prepare ourselves for a radical change. Where there is a will these is a way. 'Will' alone determines whether one suceeds or fails. Life or death? Admiration or insults? Victory or defeat? All these are in our own hands. *Srimad Bhagavad* (6th chapter, 5th sloka) states:

उद्धरे-दात्मनात्मांन नात्मान-मवसादयेत्......

One should raise oneself through the self, and never lower oneself; for the self alone is one's friend and the self alone is one's enemy.

Here let me narrate a small story to stress the above point.

Boy: Is the insect alive or dead?
Saint: It is in your hands.
(Here the saint means that the decision to keep the insect alive or kill it is in the boy's hands.)

A small boy who wanted to demean a wise saint caught a small butterfly. He kept it in his palm and hid his hand is his pant pocket. He went to the wise saint (whom he could not tolerate) and asked, "O wise saint! People from all walks of life admire your wisdom. Can you use your wisdom and tell me whether the insect in my pant pocket is dead or still alive?"

If the saint said 'dead' he wanted to release the butterfly alive and prove him wrong; on the other hand, if the saint said that it was 'alive' he wantd to crush and kill the insect and again prove the saint wrong. Either way he wantd to make to saint look a liar and cut a sorry figure.

The wise saint was too smart and simply said, "It is in your hands."

Our life is also like the life of that butterfly. It is in our hands. Every decision which determines our victory or defeat is in our own hands, our own will. If there is a will, there is a way!

Aim for the Peak

Some people were enjoying the scenic site near a pond. There were numerous lotus flowers in full bloom on the surface of the pond which everybody appreciated. A wise man was in deep thought. He was thinking about the length of the lotus. Will it be two feet? Or four feet? How much will it be? Then suddenly it struck him.

A lotus by itself has no length or height. The depth of water is the height of a lotus. A smile like the full bloom of a lotus appeared on his face. If the level of water in the pond is two feet, the lotus stands above it. If the water level increases to 20 feet, the lotus stands above it.

What is the peak in your life ? If an actor decides on the price in the movie industry and the producer pays it, that means he is at his peak. On the other hand, if the price of an actor is decided by another (producer or director) that means he has lagged behind in his field. For a speaker (who cannot quote a price as high as a movie star) if thousands of people come to hear his speech he is at peak.

One should aii for the peak in one's chosen field.

The concept of peak remains the same but its interpretation changes according to the field.

Whatever may be the field one should always aim for the peak. If a person has the motivation to reach the peak in his chosen field he is bound to reach it.

We know that as the water level rises, the lotus also goes up (in a water body). What can raise us? Thoughts! Only when our thoughts are raised, can we attain a higher level.

The level of water determines the level of the lotus. Similarly, in our life only the level of thoughts determine our position. A person with high, refined, good and sensible thoughts will achieve a high status in life and a person with low thoughts (cheap, evil) will never attain anything in life and will be at the lowest strata.

The height of the lotus in a pond is determined by the depth of the water in the pond. Similarly, your 'thoughts' determine your position in society. If you have high, refined thoughts, with a high degree of clarity, nothing can stop you from achieving what you want.

'Giving' elevates you and ' taking' takes you to a lower level. The very thought of charity, of giving something to somebody elevates you and the thought of taking something from some-body takes you to a lower level. Evil thought is as evil as the deed, says the *Bible*. Similarly a good thought is as good as a good deed. We appreciate all those who contribute so generously to hospitals, orphanages and educational institutions. On the other hand, a person who

The thought of giving is always superior to the thought of taking.

takes 'bribe' is shunned by the entire society. This is the difference between 'giving' and 'taking'. For the thoughts of giving and thoughts of taking translate into deeds. A broad outlook on life, healthy thoughts and bold perspective make a person confident which gives rise to motivation. Well motivated persons consider even an ordinary chair to be a throne. They break the shackles of narrow-minded views move on to broader horizons. They break all the hurdles, boundaries and reach the peak.

It is very important to develop confidence. This confidence must be used as a stepping stone to achieve whatever one desires. One should completely ignore the remarks of cheap-minded people who may try their level best to undermine this confidence. Our aim should be to develop thoughts which will help us achieve what we want to do.

Life is a marathon and one has to develop positive thoughts of 'winning' and have high levels of motivation to complete this "long distance foot race." Just as a marathon tests one's endurance, life challenges a person with many impossible situations and tests a person's capacity and capability to tackle them. Only positive thoughts can make us win this marathon. Our aim should be to attain the top position in this marathon.

No Inertia Please !

As long as there is blood circulation in our body we are hale and healthy. If there is any block in this circulation, for example, in coronary artery (which supplies blood to the heart) there is a heart attack, the first alarming signal impending death.

The earth rotates around its axis and this causes morning and night; it revolves around the sun and this brings about the various climatic changes, like rains, summer and winter. We see thus that the motion of earth sustains life in this earth. Not only earth, all the planets are in constant motion. Motion is their first and foremost duty.

The rivers which are moving water bodies have given rise to cities and civilisations. The rivers which have moving water sustains life, and a stagnant river breeds mosquitoes and bacteria.

Like a stream of blood, like a planet, like a river a human being by nature is meant to be dynamic active, energetic, vital. A human being is supposed to be always in an active, go ahead mode. If any individual plans to be in inertia the world discards him like a wastepaper.

This world has been conceived to function as a *karma-bhoomi'* where everybody has to function . A person has no right to be in this world if he prefers to be in inertia. An existence with inertia is worse than even non-existence It is the duty of every individual to shun lassitude and inertia and be active and productive.

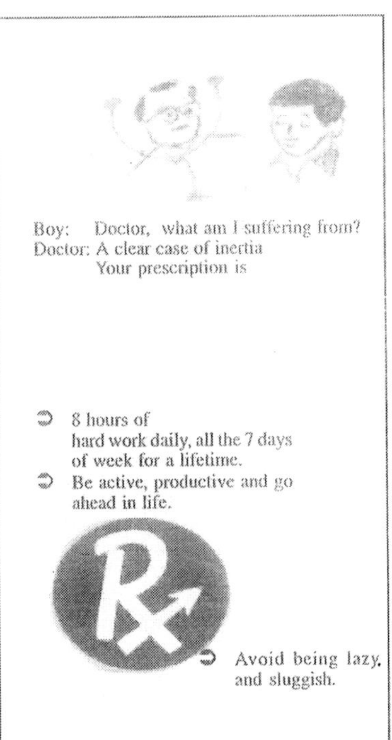

One can learn the lesson of hard work and get motivated from the elders living in villages. Even in old age most of them get up early in the morning and work according to their capacity. Everybody tries to be active, productive and useful. For them hard work serves as food, as relaxation, and sustains their life.

The American millionaire Rockfeller used to work hard even in his old age. His philosophy was, "One should work hard to come up in life and having achieved this must work harder to sustain and maintain the success. If a person stops working after achieving something he is bound to lose his success. Hard work is not only for money but also for good health and a peaceful mind."

For anybody who wants happiness, peace of mind, healthy body and money, the two most important points to remember are:

1) hard work, be productive, be active.

2) no inertia please!

****

3

Emulate Winners

People who want to win in this marathon of life must closely watch the winners and learn from their experiences. Personal observation or contact with winners can teach one a lot of lessons on life and how to win the various challenges offered by life. Knowledge or skill gained from such lessons can affect will and improve one's outlook and performance.

There is a lot of difference between looking and observing. One should closely observe (not look) at the winners. Such keen observation alone will motivate you. Along with Mahatma

Gandhi hundreds of others also saw the play 'Harishchandra'. But only Gandhiji learnt the importance of 'Truth' from the play. This is because he was observing and others were merely watching the play. Motivation comes from keen observation and learning.

Most of the winners have the following qualities:

a) Hardworking nature

b) 'Try Try Try again' mentality.

c) Deep enthusiasm, devotion, interest in their field of excellence.

Such qualities should be imbibed by the prospective winners. There is nothing called failure in life. It is a minor setback which is mistaken as failure. The failures cannot appreciate the great qualities of the winners and attribute it to Luck, God's partial grace. (God can never be partial. He is always impartial), favourable plantary positions, a great horoscope, luck lines in the palm, etc., instead of the success of the winners who have in fact achieved their success by of dint of sheer hard work.

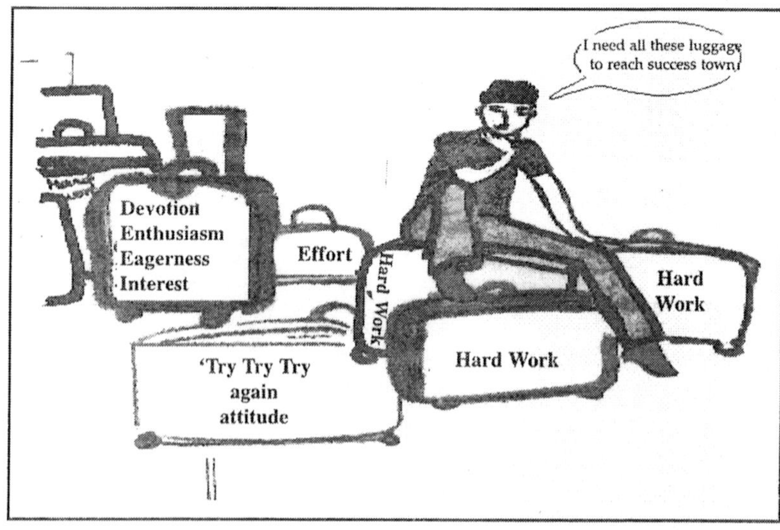

God helps those who help themselves and He rewards each person according to his/her efforts. God by nature is kind, benevolent but a man too must work hard. In this cyber age with computers, electronic and digital gadgets doing everything, man's efforts have become a rare commodity to find.

The world-renowned musical genius (who could not hear) attributed his success to playing the piano for eight hours of daily practice. When somebody complimented his talent as a rare gift of God he corrected it by saying that "Practice can give such a talent to anybody." One should never equate hard work to luck. This is outrageous.

Avoid Pessimism

Some people have a pessimistic attitude. They have a preconceived notion that everything is going against them, everything they are attempting is going to fail invariably. They blame every situation, every person for sabotaging their ideas and efforts. Something which might have occurred as a coincidence becomes a source of constant worry to such people. Such negative attitude breeds pessimism and ultimately thwarts one's progress and success in future attempts.

Have you seen the halo of light surrounding the heads of great spiritual leaders in their pictures or paintings? This is called 'Aura'. This bright atmosphere surrounding a person represents mental strength, clarity of thought, majesty, equipoise, powerful positive vibrations and optimism. We must be able to imbibe such qualities. 'Nip the evil in the bud' goes the saying. One should immediately nip the pessimism in one's mind before it tries to destroy one's psyche.

God's grace and positive vibrations can be imbibed only when a person is receptive. If he is going to be filled with negative thoughts or pessimism, he will not be able to receive the positive attributes. A broadminded receptive mind can capture all the positive vibrations and optimism pervading this universe.

One can apply the concept of 'rain water harvesting' here. Suppose the catchment areas are blocked with dirt, mud and rubbish, not a single drop of pouring rain can be saved. On the other hand, if these catchment areas are clean and ready to receive the rainwater without any blockage, a lot of rain water can be saved and utilised when needed. Similarly, a clean mind can capture and trap a lot of optimism; such a mind paves way for success. Our mind should replay the happy, positive incidents like a CD player again and again. Positive, happy incidents remembered, replayed, again and again leads to consolidation of positive energy. This cumulative accumulation of positive energy can result in huge success. Many winners have used this strategy.

The power of positive thinking

1. The mind replays and recollects a positive event. Here it is getting admission to study law to learn the science of justice.

2. Over a peiod of time these positive thoughts produce a cumulative effect. The mind begins to make predictions. Here it is the person who after completing his law studies becomes a successful lawyer.

3. The mind has now acquired the power to make things happen. The successful conditioning of the mind has made it capable of doing great things. Here it is the lawyer who with his optimism has become a judge!

This mind is unique. Like a video or audio instrument it first records the various incidences a person undergoes. Later it gets transformed into a magical instrument. The mind which records the past events begins to make future predictions—what may or may not happen! The mind on its basis of past events begins to predict the future events. This 'magical capacity' of mind becomes strange in the days to come and begins to 'make' such events happen! From mere prediction the mind begins to operate. From 'can happen intuition' the mind makes it happen! When the mind is undergoing this transformation one should be vigilant. Such vigilant individuals become winners!

One should never attach importance to certain coincidences which may seem to work against us. For example, a person who has prepared well for his exams may get fever on the day of the exam, on the day of marriage, or at the death of a close relative. These should be taken in one's stride. We should never encourage the negative thoughts that something or somebody is working against us. Everything and everybody in this universe are functioning harmoniously. Everything is favourable to everybody. This should be the perspective towards life.

Beware of Your Adversary

The world is made up of both favourable and unfavourable attributes. Actually there is nothing called unfavourable; it lies in the way we look at a particular aspect. A winner sees favourable attributes even in a so-called unfavourable aspect.

Let us assume that a 'person' is the ruling party (or party in power). The world then should not be considered the opposition party (always planning things against the party in power). The worldAfter observing try to imbibe the winning qualities*Observe the winners.*

There is a lot of difference between mere looking and observing is 'the general body' of the ruling party. It has both supporters and adversaries.

Some individuals have this habit of blowing even a small thing out of proportion. They magnify even small setbacks as big failures. Their favourite lines are:

"I have lost all hope."

"I am dejected."

"I have given up hope."

"I have lost all faith."

"It's gone forever."

Some make a mountain act of a molehill. "It has left a deep scar on my heart." It is possible for one to assault you physically

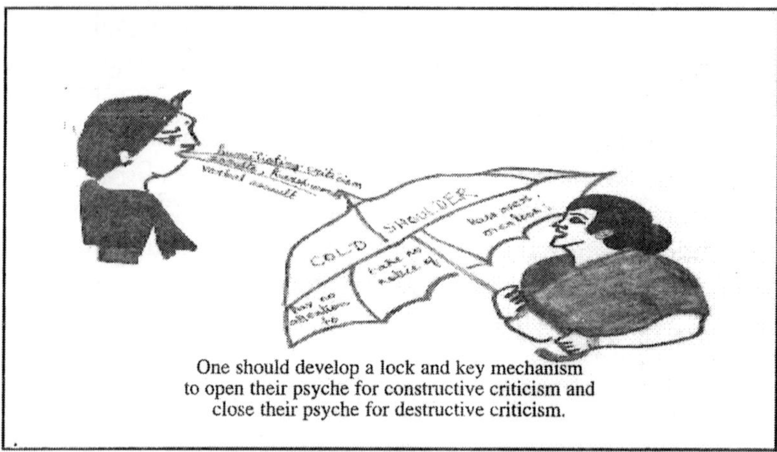

One should develop a lock and key mechanism to open their psyche for constructive criticism and close their psyche for destructive criticism.

without your permission but one cannot assault you psychologically (mentally) unless you want to get assaulted out of your own will. Your adversary cannot insult you, malign you, humiliate or harm you unless you want to get all these out of your own will. You cannot be so weak as to surrender your 'psyche' completely to them. One should design a 'lock and key' mechanism to open one's psyche to appreciation, positive criticism and inspiring words and close one's psyche to insults, negative criticism and useless back biting.

When your adversary tries to assault you verbally he is intending to harm your psyche. If you are going to pave the way for his intention you are letting him win. Just brush aside his 'verbal assault' and he will be forced to learn his lesson.

The great spiritual leader, Swami Vivekananda, was once

insulted by some men who thought he didn't know proper English. But when they listened to his refined English speech they were struck with shame. They asked Swami why he was not angry with their insults. Swami smiled and replied, "I am not meeting fools for the first time." How nicely he gave them a fitting reply.

Prospective winners should adopt this kind of attitude against their adversaries. The rule is "My adversary is trying to harm my psyche by verbal assaults and I am not going to fall a prey to his intentions." This kind of attitude motivates a person to go ahead in his pursuit of goal and ignore stupid, cheap gossip from his adversary. Ignoring such verbal attacks makes the enemy learn his lesson. Failure to evoke anger makes him pack his bag of insults and leave, never to cross your path again.

****

4
Confidence-building Measures

Give up Masochism

Masochism means 'pleasure in suffering pain'. Such masochistic individuals wallow in 'self-pity'. They create situations that make them suffer and have self-pity and pleasure out of suffering. You should avoid such masochistic individuals who do not motivate you.

When a 'winner to be' takes up a project and is enthusiastically forming a 'team' to work on the project, masochists say, 'Carry on with the project. I can't be a part of your team." The 'winner to be' also gets affected by the despondency of such 'self-pity' craving individuals leading to non-motivation.

Such masochistic individuals can be grouped into two categories: (1) those with superiority complex considering themselves too superior to be placed in a 'substandard' project team (2) 'inferiority complex' and plagued masochists who deny themselves the opportunity of working in a team and getting experience and inspiration from the others. They feel they are inferior in talent and capacity and do not fit in the team. They end up killing the joy and enthusiasm of the 'team to be' and also feel as if their sorrow and despair are linked to their happiness and zest. When the superiority complex or the inferiority complex is not linked to masochism it can be changed, and such individuals can be motivated. Masochistic individuals use their weapons of tears, dejection, desperation, depression, misery, self-pity, despondency, hopelessness to kill not only their own joy but also the motivation of people around them.

Tears which are shed out of achievement, success and hard work are precious but tears out of self-pity and induced suffering are not worth a penny.

There is a Silver Lining in Every Cloud

"If only I had a fair skin, I would have looked pretty too," complain girls.

"If only I had been a bit more taller, I could have become a police officer," complain so many guys.

"If I had been born on 'that date', 'that star', 'that zodiac sign' my luck would have been so great. The astrologer predicted this..." complain so many people.

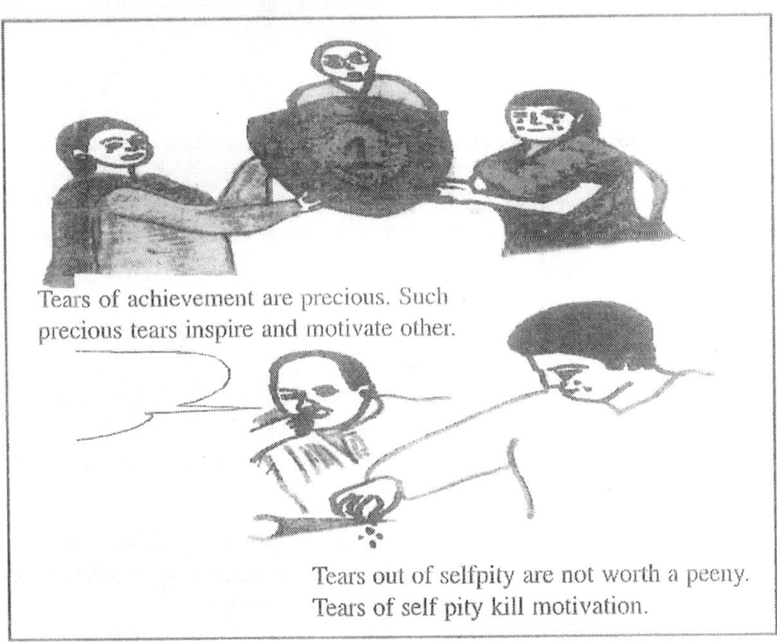

Tears of achievement are precious. Such precious tears inspire and motivate other.

Tears out of selfpity are not worth a peeny. Tears of self pity kill motivation.

'If I had', 'If only...', 'But for my...', – such complaints are not worth a penny.

One can utilise what one has and can achieve the peak in any field. An industry can increase the production by making use of the available raw materials. Similarly, an individual can use his available potential and talents and can achieve his goal. He should avoid justifying his setbacks by blaming what he doesn't have. This is escapism.

Height, complexion, appearance, family background, social status—if a person doesn't have these it is stupid to be crying over it. The absence of all these can still make you succeed. This is the message that God is trying to give us! He has given us an opportunity to prove that we can succeed in spite of having none of these attributes.

A girl who is not fit may not become a beauty queen but she can definitely become a judge in a beauty contest! A man who is not tall enough to qualify for a police job can become a district collector who can command even a police officer!

A person who may have been born in a 'not so good' star or date, an inauspicious time, can prove the astrologer wrong by achieving what seems impossible to astrology.

If a person has the will to succeed, if he has the 'nothing can defeat me' attitude even his minus points become plus points. Every cloud has a silver lining. There are two kinds of 'I don't have' in life:

1. Modifiable I don't haves.
2. Non-modifiable I don't haves.

God has graced every individual to use his power of discretion to decide what is modifiable and what cannot be. A person must carefully see his positive and negative points. He must be able to use his discretion and see whether his negativities are modifiable, whether they can be changed. If so he must try to change them to his advantage.

If he feels his negative points cannot be changed he should stop worrying and complaining about it. Sometimes this negative point can be used as a stepping stone to success. 'Disadvantage' can be turned to 'advantage'. Hrithik Roshan with his perfect 'Adonis' looks has given only two hits whereas Shah Rukh Khan with his 'not so perfect looks' has been giving hit movies one after another. Govinda, with a slightly plump body, has exceptional dancing skills which make him popular.

Sudha Chandran lost her leg in an accident. She accepted the fact, got on artificial limb fixed and succeeded in giving dance performances! Her grit and determination have motivated millions of people. What a healthy man with both his legs intact cannot do, she can do with one leg. Though she lost a leg, she did not lose her courage and determination. It is pathetic to see so many youngsters who have everything but have lost their motivation and courage. A leg removed by amputation can be replaced with an artificial limb but motivation lost cannot be replaced by any prosthesis unless the person himself gets remotivated by his own efforts.

One should never care about one's defects in appearance or body. If something can be corrected by a plastic surgery or an artificial implant you can resort to it. If not' one should accept it and learn to live with it. A person can become handicapped physically but this should not lead to a mental handicap.

Hindu mythology mentions about a great saint Ashtavakrar who had eight bends in his body. With all these defective bends, ignoring taunts from others, with great difficulty in walking he mastered all the four *Vedas* and became a wise *pundit*. Such should be the spirit and determination!

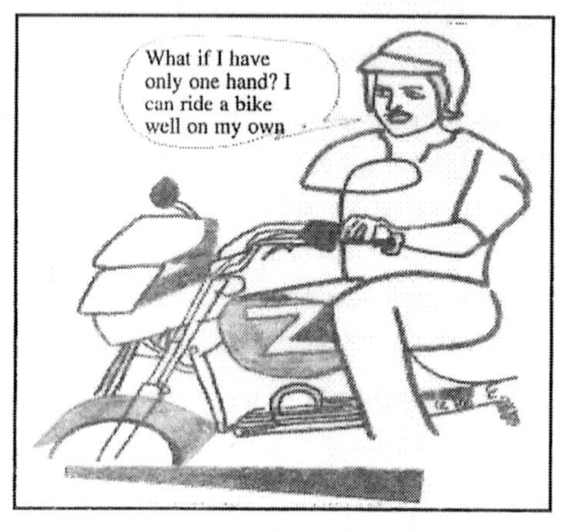

If only a person can learn to use his defects to his advantage, his success can inspire and motivate so many others.

Expectations and Disappointments

We all expect something from others. We expect some change, some adaptation or adjustment from people around. This expectation can be as drastic as a complete 'metamorphosis' or a 'minor alteration'— in attitude, behaviour or innate nature.

A boss may expect some radical change in the performance of his subordinate. A husband may like to see a drastic change in his wife's temperament. There is nothing wrong in all these but one should expect the change for good. Changes cannot occur in a day. It has to be slow, progressive and gradual.

A person should build his dream castle on the basis of expectations he has from others. The expectation will be on the part of others also. He should be aware of this. What right does he have to say, "He should be like this, not like that." When the expectations are not fulfilled a person feels frustrated, disappointed and stressed.

Not only in the family or office, our expectations are also from every aspect of society. Starting from a taxi driver, shopkeeper, bank employee to God our expectations are that they should be fair in every dealing. We want the entire society to be made of mother Teresas, Gandhijis, Buddhas and saints. There is nothing wrong in such expectations, for such changes to happen, but you should act, not merely think.

A man doesn't crop up like a mushroom. Over a period of time his birth, family upbringing, education, social standing all condition him to what he is. His experiences all create 'him' by influencing his personality. It is not possible to change a man in a second, at the drop of a hat. One should realise that each man is different from another. No two men can agree or disagree in anything and everything like automatic clones. We must accept these differences in attitudes among people. Over-expectation will lead to disappointments. Only some can 'change' according to the need and 'grow' dynamically. Very few can change with the radical changes happening around them. Many conservatives prefer to stay as they are. The fast changing world has no time for them. If they have no motivation to change for the better, they remain behind in this race of progress, change and advancement.

External environment may change but not the internal mental make-up for many conservative non-progressive individuals. We often fail in such endeavours. You may put a hundred digital computers around them but they will still like to do their calculation with an abacus! No amount of prompting will change their internal stubborn nature.

You cannot change anything in this world except one person and his attitude — and that is You! You can change for better by your own efforts. First apply the change you expect from others to yourself. Try to achieve this change, and it will make a big difference!

****

5

Discover Yourself

Everybody in this world wants to meet either a popular person or a social celebrity. Similarly, everyone wants to avoid those whom they dislike or can't tolerate. We are all very eager in meeting somebody whom we admire. We feel annoyed on meeting someone whom we dislike.

Why do we want to meet someone eagerly? Either we get a lot of happiness on meeting him/her or we get motivated on seeing them. We also feel proud on meeting somebody whom we consider to be great.

Some get peace on meeting spiritual leaders. Some want to promote their ideas by meeting somebody popular in their field of expertise; fans go mad on meeting their favourite movie or pop star whom they worship.

We are all keen to meet a celebrity but we have never given any thought of meeting one important person who really matters. Meeting this person can change your life. You even avoid meeting him when situations arise and bring him face to face with you. You try to escape when we meet him. But 'he' really matters. Can you guess? He is no one but your own-self!

Yes! You must meet the real You! There can be a womaniser inside a so-called 'saint'. There can be a 'male chauvinist' inside an author who may write exclusively on 'women's liberation'.

There can be a 'ferocious carnivore' who claims to be a lover of animals and a strict vegetarian. But in all these cases the real person never manifests, only the facade is evident. One must never avoid the eye contact with the real inner self. The real inner self is the truth. The external facade is a 'make up'. Your real inner self alone can judge you. Please meet him. Initially the facade is to hide the real inner-self from others; later it becomes a cloak to conceal the inner self from your own self.

We seem to project a 'stranger' to the people around us. The real 'we' never comes out. You must first recognise the real identity hiding within you, then meet yourself with outstretched hands. This alone can make you take a step towards success. To

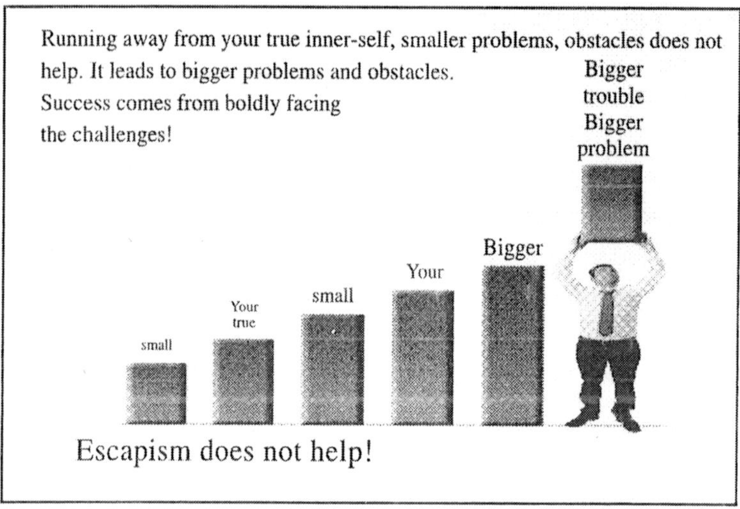

Escapism does not help!

meet the 'real self' you have to take an 'internal tour'— introspect and examine your own thoughts and feelings. In doing this you may have to fumble, grope about, tumble, but dont give up! Only when the 'gap' between the 'true self' and 'projected self' vanishes success and motivation begin to materialise.

You should not hide behind false religious rituals or

superstitious practices to avoid meeting the real 'self'. This kind of escapism helps nothing. You should shake out the fear, meet the real 'self', get motivated and start progressing towards your goal.

While praying to God your prayer should be "Oh God! Give me enough strength and courage to face the obstacles and problems in front of me. Let me win in my ventures."

Your prayer should not be "oh God! Let me not have any problem." This prayer is sheer cowardice and paves the way for an escapism mentality.

Challenges, problems, obstacles in life should be tackled with skill, motivation and courage. This makes life interesting. Avoiding or running away from a problem complicates and aggravates the already existing problem.

1. Face the problem and win it — winner's strategy
2. Escape and augment the problem—looser's formula. The choice should be (1) and success is guaranteed.

Concentrate on Your Subconscious State

We often use some tactics to avoid people whom we dislike (and would like to avoid at any cost), hiding behind a tree on seeing them at a distance, using a newspaper or cap to cover our face to avoid being seen by them, etc. These tactics are harmless.

There are some people who want to avoid their inner-self. They run away from their self! An alcoholic who is always in an inebriated state may justify his habit by saying, "I want to forget myself, my problems." Such an argument is utter foolishness. These kinds of addictions lead to mere problems and confusions. Drug addicts, smokers, who also belong to a similar category are all cheating themselves by using escapisms. They can be termed as temporary suicide. Self-esteem, self-respect are needed for a person to get rid of these habits.

Psychiatry divides mind into two states: conscious and

subconscious. In the awake state, the conscious mind records various data regarding age, gender, social status, academic qualifications, etc. The various facial expressions (which are like 'magical masquerades', 'pretence') are all products of the conscious mind.

The subconscious mind doesn't relate to the conscious mind. As the interval or gap between these two states of mind increases the person begins to experience confusion, and he loses peace of mind. When these states of mind turn inimical, he may even turn into a mentally disturbed individual. He may show various signs and symptoms of psychological illness.

A person can become mere refined, superior and a better human being if he decreases the gap between conscious and subconscious states of the mind. This diminished gap between the two states of mind can improve the person's merit. He becomes a commendable, admirable individual. Understanding this concept can change one's life for the better.

We have all projected only our conscious aspect as our personality. The world has seen only our projected conscious state as our identity. In truth our 'subconscious' is the true reflection of our inner self. Our subconsious state needs our scrutiny. The subconscious state (which is our true self) is a Pandora's box. Nobody knows what it contains.

Our subconscious mind may have treasures or skeletons. Sometimes it is a treasure-chest and sometimes it is a garbage can. Our true inner self is sometimes a "Buddha"; sometimes the inner self turns into a "cold-blooded killer". The subconscious mind may thus represent a "cold-blooded killing Buddha"; a 'spiritual butcher'. Our true inner self may thus be a wise but brutal character. But the special attribute maintains a check on the vicious attribute. Like a kaleidoscope which produces changing patterns with mirrors and coloured fragments this subconscious mind too changes patterns of characteristics. It may be a pig turning into a deer. The true inner self can be a present coal but it is a future diamond. The subconscious mind appears as on ordinary stone on a cursory look but the trained eye (like that of a sculptor) can make out a fine statue or fine piece of sculpture with it.

You have to start working on this subconscious mind. It has tremendous potential lying dormant in it. Once you begin to sculpt your subconscious mind it will begin to sculpt your personality, bringing out the unexplored facets of talents and hidden potential in you. When a sculptor becomes an expert in carving sculptures, both the sculptor and the sculpture complement each other. If the sculptor sculpts a statue to perfection, the statue too complements him by making him win awards and accolades. Thus you must start concentrating on your subconscious mind. As you begin to sculpt your subconscious mind, the undeveloped and unrealised latent capabilities of this mind will begin to sculpt your personality. It will be a give and take process.

You sculpt the subconscious mind, and the subconsious mind will sculpt your personality.

You must remember that every man has both positive and negative attributes in him. It is up to him to train his subconscious mind, suppress or completely abolish the harmful traits and evolve/augment his positive traits. Work on the strong points and ignore the weak points in your personality. Here it is important to remember that some weak points in a person may be a boon in disguise. They may even help in amplifying or boosting the strong points by remaining feeble. Isn't it true that "strong loops of a chain are held by weak links and the strength of the chain lies in these weak links!"

Estimating One's Nature

Unless a person has wrong thoughts in his subconscious mind his actions cannot go wrong. An interesting point here is that even the person concerned is unaware of harbouring such wrong thoughts in his (subconscious) mind, i.e., the conscious mind is unaware of the subconsious thoughts!

This is precisely the reason why we cannot believe some of our own actions. We end up doing something totally unrelated to our nature and then wonder, 'How could I do it?' The same thing applies to our unexposed talents. Sometimes we achieve something great and we ourselves cannot believe our potential. In *Mahabharata* there are many instances where Yudhishtira—'integrity and morality personified'— gives a glimpse of his 'faults and flaws'. Duryodhana, the 'evil incarnate', had some fine qualities which again manifests in some instances in the *Mahabharata.* Again these are nothing but the play of the subconscious mind.

We all inherit so many genetic traits from our ancestors. The beautiful eyes of an ancestral aunt can be inherited by a newborn niece. She may also inherit a not so beautiful disease or defect of the same aunt. She may not inherit any of these. This is also a possibility. Artistic talent or killer instinct can be inherited by genes. All these happen without one's knowledge, and our subconscious mind is unable to give an explanation for many of these traits.

Hindu philosophy and texts attribute the concept of reincarnation to these. When a person dies and is reborn his spirit records various good and bad experiences of his past births. These recorded experiences function as the subconscious mind. Whatever be the explanation one can never categorically classify an individual as a good or bad person. One has to judge a person by calculating the percentage of each attribute. If the percentage of good attributes is more, he is labelled good or else he is labelled a bad person. A man is a mixture of strengths and weaknesses. There is something very vulnerable inside every strong or hard personality, and something very tough and indestructible inside a feeble personality.

Nothing can make a strong, solid iron pillar fall but soft flakes of rust can make it collapse. In many cases strong external forces become useless but a small internal push can make things happen. Similarly the good or bad instincts from our subconscious motivate or dishearten our spirits.

****

6

Multifaceted

A man has many faces. Yudhishtira had an evil side to his flawless character and Duryodhana had a dignified side to his evil nature. We all have multiple faces. Apart from the one face (physical) which stands on our neck, we have 'many' hidden faces. All these faces project our different traits, characters and shades.

We are influenced by many persons. We also get influenced by books, movies, certain incidents, experiences and lectures. All these have a profound effect on us and bring out new faces in us. Suppose you are an actor. You will be seeing shades of every popular actor in your action, style, dialogue delivery and body language. This is because you are inspired and influenced by them, consciously or unconsciously. Along with being an actor, if you are an avid reader of books of a particular author, you begin to exhibit certain characteristics of that author or his books—his way of thinking, his choice of words, his way of taking decisions or the book's way of dealing with certain situations. You may be somebody's son, husband and father. So the influences also come from parents, wife, children. You were once a student, so the teacher's influence too is there. The persons who influence you begin to have a bearing on you. The impact they create in your psyche manifests in your personality.

The effect of such an impact can be extremely useful if it is going to evoke motivation in you. Such motivation can affect, alter and change your thinking and bring about success in your all endeavours.

Our personality is like a collage. Imagine a picture made by gluing pieces of paper on a backing. Similarly, the different people who influence and inspire us with their traits, mannerisms and characteristics are glued together to form our personality. When seen from one angle one aspect shines brightly, and when seen from the other side a different aspect comes out. Take the example of Ravana, the villain of the epic, the Ramayana. He had so many faces literally (he had 10 faces) but his personality was so multifaceted.

1. We all known him as a womaniser—who abducted Sita—this is only one of his single facet (a womaniser).
2. Ha was a great devotee of Lord Shiva ('devotion' is exhibited).
3. He lifted the Kailash Mountain with all his strength (valour is exhibited).
4. He could play the veena (here his musical talent is exhibited).

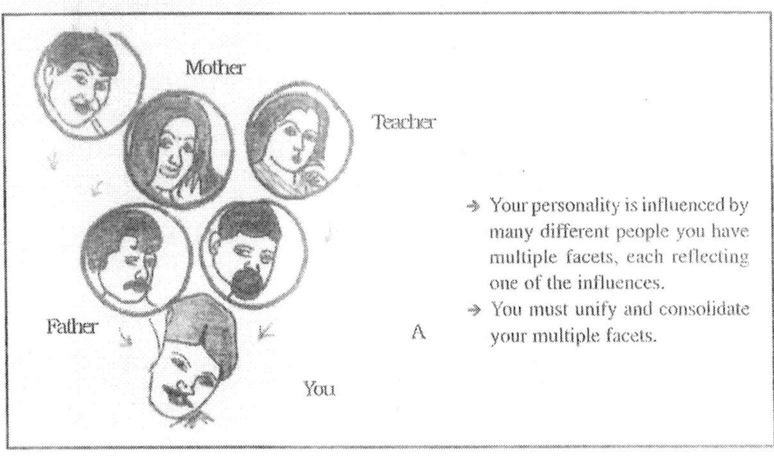

5. He had great affection for his brothers and sisters (here we see his loving nature).

All these 'facets' of Ravana could never be consolidated. They were all like loose ends never combined, never secured into a strong force. Lord Rama, on the other hand, could combine all his multiple facets—his valour, love and affection, kindness, skills, devotion, duty-bound nature into one single consolidated entity— and that was 'integrity'. Rama stands for integrity and vanquished Ravana in the war.

You must be able to consolidate the various facets of personality in you. You must destroy the evil facets, augment the good traits. Such unification of various facets will bring about a equipoise in mind which can guide you like a torchlight (in dark) to carry on in your path of achievement and ultimately reach the goal you had aspired for.

The 'Coalition' Confusion

A coalition government is always a source of confusion and conflict. Every human being is a coalition government in himself. We are all a product of coalition of the body and life. 'Body + Life' constitutes a live human being. The body again is a coalition of bones, nerves, flesh, blood, skin; the genes which constitute the genetic material or make up of our body is formed by coalition of DNA, RNA, etc. Each cell of our body has this coalition. The body+life coalition constitutes not only being 'alive' but also the 'mind'. The mind controls both the body and life. The mind records various events relating to the body and life. Every human being has three recorded data in his body.

1. Genetic data—which carries traits, disease potential, etc., of the individual. Genetic science is studying this genetic data and has mapped various genes controlling various characteristics.

2. Data recorded by 'life. This constitutes various experiences recorded by life. Here we have to mention about the Hindu philosophy which says life records various experiences and

this data is carried from one birth to another. These don't surface as the individual is ignorant of carrying such data within him. These are often exhibited is some form from our not so well explored subconscious mind.

3. Data recorded by mind. Psychology has studied this in detail. Hindu philosophy however mentions this briefly. These data are restricted to that 'present' birth only. It is not carried to the next incarnation.

These three data form a coalition inside each one of us. The conflicts, confusions and turmoils we experience are due to the various ups and downs in this coalition. The powerful leader of a coalition should have a control on his various parties. He must be firm and take a strong view on all decisions, otherwise the coalition will topple. If each party in a coalition begins to have its own stand, there will be no union in the coalition. The same principle applies to 'coalition' in an individual. There should be a union of body, life and mind (well established equilibrium). All the three must be at peace with each other and work harmoniously.

Modern science agrees on genetic data (relating to the body) and data recorded by the mind but the life recorded data is not acceptable. The theory of incarnation and reincarnation does not gel with modern science. Not only Hindu philosophy but even Buddhist and Jain texts also agree on reincarnation and life recorded experiences. Lord Rama and Lord Krishna are both considered as incarnations of Narayana. Rama in one incarnation becomes Krishna in the next. Here one must remember that they had all taken human forms. So when 'human ' parlance comes even the supreme beings carry life experiences into succeeding births Archaeological evidences have proven the existence of Rama, Krishna,.etc. No amount of convincing can satisfy the scientists.

There are two important points:

1. Modern science agrees about two datas in our body.
   i) Genetic data (imprinted in each cell of our body)
   ii) Mind related data (psychology studies this)
2. Spiritual science mentions a data related to life — its experiences how it is recorded birth after birth, each birth carrying some data (in the form of actions, deeds, etc.) into the next birth.

These three entities motivate us and make us do many things. They also subdue us, demotivate us and stop us from doing various things. One should align these three into a perfect harmonious state and go in pursuit of one's goals.

The success of a coalition government lies in perfect alignment of the various parties in it. The other important factors for its success are a strong, firm leader and perfect understanding between the various parties. The association aspect of a coalition party is meant for a common purpose association formed for a mutual benefit. These aspects also apply for the coalition in an individual between the three entities mentioned above. The coalition should work in a constructive mode and not in a destructive mode. The individual should be aware of this important axiom.

The 'Living' Trash

Have you ever seen a wastepaper basket worth eight thousand rupees? I have seen it. My friend's office desk is eight thousand rupees worth garbage can. He is forever in search of something on his office desk—his keys, rail ticket, purse, tablets—he is always searching for something. He never puts anything in order. Utter entropy prevails in the drawers and on his desk top. His wife goes one step further! She buys a packet of salt every-day as she never places the salt in its proper bottle on the kitchen shelf. She ends up searching for it every day, gets bored, buys a new packet to make things easy! Their house has everything but nothing in its proper place. The only astonishing fact is the presence of 'alive' rubbish in that can.

Now-a-days even garbage serves as raw material for harnessing electricity. Bio-degradable wastes turn into manure for plants and crops. Cacti the and weeds are weeded out as rubbish but if they grow on the borders of the field they serve as a fence! A protection for the crops in the field.

What we have doesn't matter, what matters is where do we have it. How we have kept it becomes the next important concern. Anything which is well maintained, well organised and well kept becomes an investment. This also makes us aware of how blessed we are. We become aware of our possessions. This motivates us and we become more confident and clear in our perceptions. Self-assurance ensues within us.

We must organise our mind just like organising a house or desk in an office. Just as the things are dusted, cleaned and arranged in their appropriate places we must organise our thoughts. Just as a shopkeeper does a stock-taking of his materials we must do a stock-taking of our thoughts.

Such an act of 'thought organisation' helps us in proper alignments of our genetic life and mind data. A cobweb in the corner of your house is ugly whereas a cobweb in the corner of your mind is dangerous. Cobwebs of ill, evil, and nasty thoughts can ruin you. Clear such cobwebs with a 'determination to succeed' duster. Throw out the rubbish of desolation, despair, dejection and hopelessness. Wash, clean, refine and polish all those faculties which emit vibrations of motivation, encouragement, confidence and success. Throw the 'failure bulbs' which have lost their use. Light the new 100 watt bulbs of success and victory.

Our mind needs to eject out the unwanted emotions of vindictive anger, (remember anger is one letter short of danger), cheap and dirty ideas, useless contempt, baseless inferiority complex, and lack of drive and determination. These are all toxins which may poison your spirit and enthusiasm. Meditation alone can help you in this process of ejecting out the negative emotions. It helps you to cogitate, muse, ponder, reflect, ruminate and think—all these are very useful. Self-evaluation and self-analysis are the first steps in meditation. We imbibe so much from external environment that we lose our internal aspect completely. Meditation aids in introspection. This has to be done by the individual himself, nobody can do it (proxy) for him. The basic principles of meditation, once learnt, need no external help. The person can do it on his own. 'Self-help is the best help'!

****

7

Self-help

Ramakrishna Paramahansa's mere touch transformed Narendra into Vivekananda. Inspired by this fact a man asked Acharya Vinoba Bhave to do the same to him. "Your mere touch can transfor me into, a wise man" said the person eagerly to Vinoba Bhave. Acharya's reply was, "If I touch you and turn you into a wise man, somebody else's touch can turn you into a fool too. If this can happen, even that can happen. On the other hand, self-awareness and self-realisation can turn you into a wise man who can never be changed into anything else. Try self-help."

Try Self-help

If somebody can construct you, somebody can destruct you too. You should remain what you are. You shouldn't become something programmed by others. This was Acharya Vinoba

Bhave's teaching. Never give up your individuality, identity and distinctive trademark for a 'mask' which others can supply you with.

Today there are many cults, organisations and spiritual gatherings in which the so-called 'Gurus' create mere fools instead of creating inspiring students. These so-called 'Gurus' in the name of motivation are creating parasites who are dependent on their Guru for everything all their life. They are unable to make any decisions on their own.

A true guru or spiritual master, after motivating his followers., teaches them the 'truth', the distinction between right and wrong. Once he is satisfied with the student's progress he may either ask the student to go and lead an independent life (using the lessons he has learnt) or may ask them to stay back to learn. A true guru may like to motivate as many students as possible and will not create parasites who cling to him like a baby dependent on its mother for everything.

In today's modern world, in the name of spiritual awakening and spiritual solutions to all problems, gullible youngsters are being taken for a ride. In the name of motivation they are brainwashed and deceived. Naive youngsters fall an easy prey to such gurus who themselves need proper awakening and enlightenment. Only God can help them! My advice to youngsters is beware of such spiritual phoneys!

Self-help is the best help. Each and every person must begin to self-evaluate and self-analyse his inner core. Introspection is very important.

Retrospection is also needed as you are able to judge yourself better, based on the findings from the past. A mirror shows your external appearance to you. Meditation can reflect your internal appearance. When a person analyses his own self, the hasty impulsive attitude is taken over by a calm, collected, composed, controlled attitude. He is able to make dispassionate decisions in a tranquil, serene state of mind. To detach yourself from the 'egoistic I' and have an objective look, give a fair, impartial view of your own faults and shortcomings. Once you master the three important exercises: self-analysis, self-evaluvation and self-help you can get motivated in the right sense and can solve any problems. We need no spiritual crutches offered by lame gurus. We can learn to be self-assertive and self-assured.

Be Your Own Critic

A mirror reflects our external appearance and a properly practised meditation reflects our internal psyche. Meditation can be done in three ways:

1. Concentration meditation.
2. Contemplation meditation.
3. Transcendental meditation.

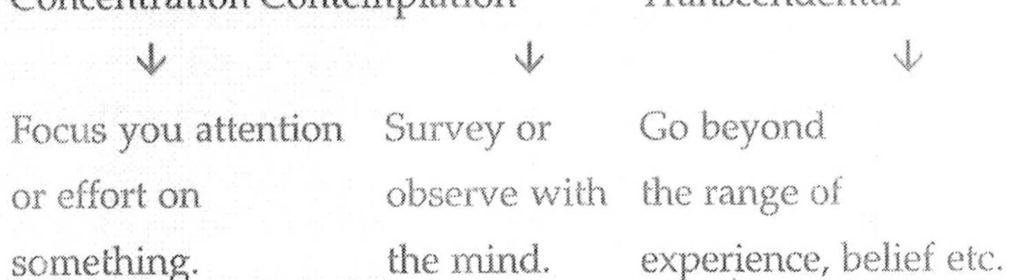

To gain anything in this world meditation is the time-tested, proven strategy. The mind which is in a dissociated, loose state, if brought to a focus, can work wonders. The mind should be focused on something, someone, some thought or a chant. The great saints and spiritual leaders who aspired for the 'Absolute' also practised meditation but their goal was different. For us, the goal is something connected to success— materialistic or position-oriented—and we need a different kind of meditation. You should not get confused between the 'aim for the Absolute (sought by sages, spiritual luninaries) and aim for the worldly things—of or concerned with earthly life or material gains (not spiritual).

In the aim for the Absolute, meditation is practised to completely make the mind a non-existent phenomenon.

Using self-analysis as water,self evaluation as fertilizer, self-help as spade one can easily get the flower of success.

For us, who are in search of motivation to achieve success in our goal, our meditation strategy is to focus our mind on something,cogitate, ruminate, think, ponder over, get into self-analysis, self-evaluation and acquire self-assurance, self-motivation and indomitable mental strength.

Remember this axiom: "For worldly success and achievements you don't need a non-existing mind. What you need is a motivated mind." This can be achieved by meditation.

A paper has the inherent capacity to get burnt and the sun has the inherent capacity to burn it. When a lens is placed between the sun and a paper it piles up the burning power. The intense heat burns the paper. Similarly, meditation acts as a lens. It piles up the loose strands of thoughts in the mind, accumulates and consolidates them into a strong focused strength and thus a man achieves immense mental strength.

Every individual must have a 'credit-debit' account of himself. The credit account of an individual must include:

* Good thoughts, good words.
* Good deeds
* Good actions
* Appreciation received from others
* Achievements

You can become your own
Critic. It helps!

My Credits

* My decision about this company was correct. Both I and the company have benefited.
* I have reached my target in profits.
* I have met my deadlines with proper planning.
* I have devoted quality time to my wife and children. They are happy.
* I thanked my subordinates for their help in this project. I should give them a bonus.
* I have played golf thrice this week; I saw a movie; read my favourite book.

My Debits

* I could not help my parents when they were in hospital.
* My boss yelled at me for not completing the pending work.
* I should not have spoiled my manager's promotional chances by speaking ill of him.
* I did not attend the parents-teacher meeting at my children's my school. They felt bad.
* I am putting on weight, my blood pressure is going up. I have not taken proper care of my health.
* I have not practised charity this year.

YOU CAN BECOME YOUR OWN CRITIC !

The debit account of the individual must include:

* Ill thoughts, bad words
* Ill deeds
* Ill actions
* Insults received from others
* Setbacks

Ponder ever your credits and debits. Retrospect like the 'rewind' switch in a CD player, rewind the past events, your past actions, thoughts, deeds. Take an objective look at all these. Just as we do a revision of our school lessons and answer papers do a revision of your past life. Be critical. Try to make corrections in the appropriate places. Criticise your various decisions and conclusions taken at various stages of life. Try to make amends. Be your own critic but let it be constructive criticism! This motivates you. You become a better judge of situations, actions, etc., in the present and the future.

You Need a Physical Balance

We correct our appearance by looking at our reflection in the mirror. Similarly, we correct our mind by reflecting on our actions, thoughts, words, deeds. This reflection is by meditation.

It is often misinterpreted that meditation is meant only for spiritual endeavours. This is not true. Meditation serves as an effective tool for motivation and helps one achieve many worldly things one may seek. There is a lot of difference between life and living. Higher spiritual goals are for those who want to win 'life'. Living refers to worldly pleasures, achievements and materialistic pursuits.

To win the concept of 'living' we need motivation, drive, stimulation, inspiration and enthusiasm. All these can be achieved by meditation.

Self-satisfaction in the case of spiritual leaders or saints means pleased with one's spiritual progress. A truly spiritual

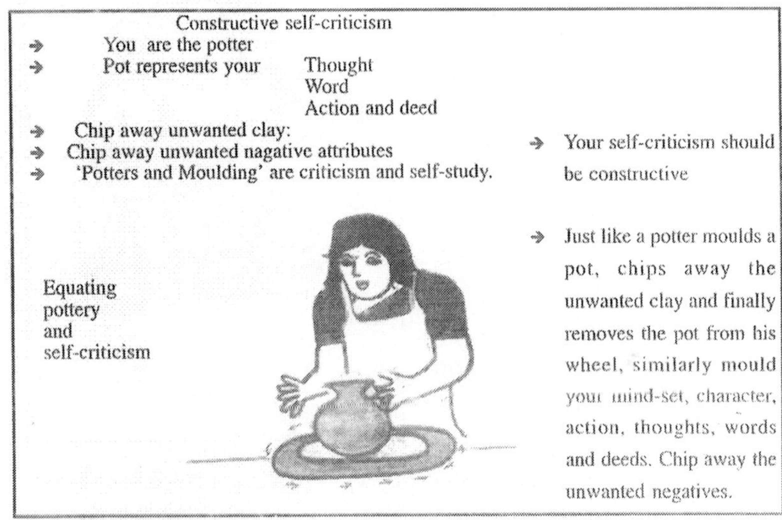

person in pursuit of the Absolute must be satisfied with his spiritual progress. There should be no conceit or pride in it.

Self-seeking attitude does not mean promoting one's selfish reasons. It should be devoid of any selfish elements. Seeking spiritual enlightenment of the self the must be the idea.

A person must give up being self-centred, being self-conscious and being selfish. He should be self-willed (not being obstinate but being determined). He should have self-control and self-assurance. He should have self-determination and self-respect.

Once these qualities are acquired and practised you can hope to reach your ultimate goal.

Each and every individual must do a self-assessment at the end of each day, of their thoughts, words and action. Like the film review in a newspaper you can critically review your thoughts, words and action of that day. Use the same 'yardstick' which you use for others to gauge your thoughts, words and actions. What applies to others applies to us also. Many of us have separate 'standards' for ourselve and others. A person who defines his nature as being brisk, quick, energetic or lively may describe someone else's as impulsive, hasty, heedless, impetuous and incautious. A person who defines his wife to be of 'social' nature may define the wife of his neighbour as a 'gossipmonger'. What is defined as being 'thrifty' nature in us may get the definition of 'miserly' nature in others. If our children speak less to the guests we admire them as being reserved and courteous; if the children of our host don't speak to us or speak less we term them as arrogant, conceited children or as morons. You should be just in assessing yourself and others. Suppose you buy a gold ornament from a shop. You weigh it in a balance and buy it. When you want to resell it, you measure it in the same balance. Consistent results come only from consistent methods. One must define, criticise, judge and acknowledge both the self and others with the same yardstick. We use the same physical balance to buy and then resell a product to ensure that the resale value matches the purchased value. Similarly, measure both your own thought-word-action and that of others with the same yardstick. Vice versa also

Use the same yardstick to assess 'self' and 'others'

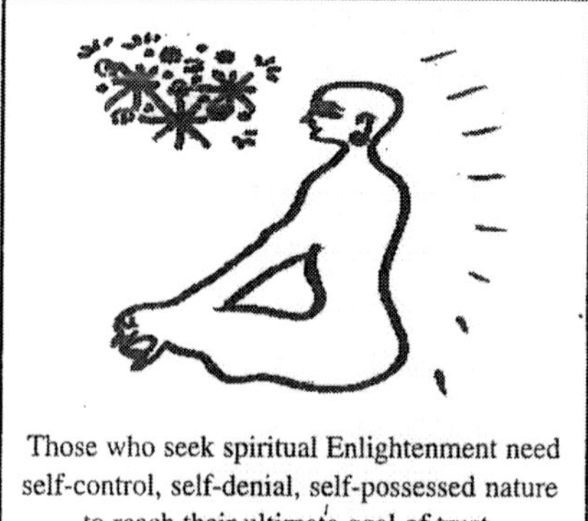

Those who seek spiritual Enlightenment need self-control, self-denial, self-possessed nature to reach their ultimate goal of trust, knowledge, bliss, absolute.

applies. Apply the same standards you apply to others to your own self.

Listing your credits and debits in nature, action, thoughts and words should be done regularly. This should become a 'data' to motivate you, to help you achieve your goals and succeed. This data should be processed and reprocessed, and the unwanted should be deleted. Whatever is necessary should be augmented and maintained and must be used as reference material to motivate and inspire us.

****

8

Time Management

Allot Some Time

All of us must allot some time daily for improving outselves—our nature, thoughts, words and action. Time management is very essential and you have to use your discretion in using the available 24 hours in a day.

If you have real concern over your will to improve then definitely you will allot some time for self-scrutiny. The 24 hours in a day are equal for everyone on this earth. Whether it is the president of the United States or a beggar in remote India, everyone has been bestowed with 24 hours in a day.

You have to manage everything in this 24 hours—work, rest, entertainment, arguments, confusion and conflicts—everything has to be accommodated in this 24 hrs.

Take the example of a coalition government. Here the leader has to allot a seat or an election ticket for every Tom, Dick and Harry in the coalition. He does it with so much dexterity that everybody is satisfied. Time management needs this kind of dexterity.

Self-analysis, self-assessment and self-improvement should take top priority in time allotment. Anything done with a passion yields excellent results. This self-improvement strategy needs passion on the part of individuals concerned. When an individual introspects and is all set to improve he needs appropriate and enough time for this exercise. This cannot be done in haste. Anything ranked appropriately in the 'priority list' automatically gets time. Have you seen a crowd paving way for a VIP when he/she enters a podium? We know that VIP's should be given priority when a thing of urgency crops up in his agenda of daily routine. So your action plan should be:

Self-analysis through self-criticism ➔ Step 1

Making a list of your plus and minus points ➔ Step 2

Constructive self-assessment ➔ Step 3

Making note of areas and scope of improvement ➔ Step 4

Action: getting down to self improvement ➔ Step 5

For all this time is in plenty if you have the passion to do it.

You are the Captain of Your Own Ship

Your are the captain of your own ship; you are the master of your own actions; you can formulate your own ways of reward and punishment methods to improve yourself. The punishment you give for your ill thoughts, bad words, wrong actions must be in such a way that it reforms and refines you. For example, you can stay away from your favourite dish, hobby or sports

YOU ARE THE CAPTAIN OF YOUR SHIP

YOU ARE THE MASTER OF YOUR FATE

Become Responsible!

Become Accountable!

Become Answerable!

for doing something wrong. A 'mental cleaning' can be prescribed—this can include helping the poor, visiting an old age home or do some act of charity. The punishment prescribed by you for your faults must be able to improve you.

Just as a punishment reforms you, a reward for your good thought-word or deed can motivate you. The thought-word-action strategy serves as a catalyst or promoter.

Meditation, breathing exercises, can all help in achieving a state of mental peace and tranquillity. Even the modern scientists advocate doing meditation, facing the north. When the electromagnetic waves from our mind up on facing the northern direction they promote mental equipoise and serenity. Sitting straight while meditating keeps your vertebral column healthy. The lungs get plenty of air. When oxygen flows the blood in our body and mind gets rejuvenated. You must select a pollution-free place to practise meditation and breath control exercises. Inspiration-retention-exhalation must be regular, not rapid. The time ratio of inspiration, retention, expiration should be 1:4:2. A therapist can be consulted before attempting such breath control exercises. Your physical condition must be 100 per cent fit to do these exercises.

Breathing is an involuntary action and most of us do not pay any attention to it. Once you make it a voluntary action you begin to have control of your ownself. Breath-control is the first step towards self-control. Breath management can slowly condition and motivate you to success management. Your breath is related to your mind. When you are emotionally hyperactive—like being angry, frustrated— your breathing also becomes rapid. Suppose you are enraged, furious, outraged or smouldering, your breathing reflects your mental turmoil. Both your heart rate and respiratory rate become rapid and irregular. The speed of mind is reflected in speed of these vital signs. The air you breathe out is hot when you are very angry whereas when you are happy and contented—when your mind is peaceful, serene, tranquil— your breathing will be like a well-oiled machine: running smoothly, regularly. The velocity of mind determines the velocity of breathing. Control breathing and you can control your mind automatically. Whenever your heart rules your mind, your right nostril breathing will be comparatively less compared to breathing from the left nostril. This will be more rapid. When your mind rules the heart the left nostril breathing will be less compared to the right nostril breathing. Therapists classify right breath as mind-related, and left breath as heart-related.

Therapists also point to a particular zone in our forehead (between eyebrows) where 'breath' remains in an equillibrium state, i.e., breath from right and left halves remain in a state of balance.

Wavelengths Must Merge

There was once a team on a visit to a waterfall. There was a movie director, engineer, diver, owner of a mineral water plant, and a washer-man. All were school friends and had come for a vacation to this beautiful picnic spot. The beautiful waterfall was the main attraction. The site of the waterfall evoked mixed reasponses from each one of them.

Movie director: I can film a beautiful romantic scene, a duet with hero and heroine in the backdrop of this waterfall.

Engineer: Electricity can be harnessed using dynamo. This waterfall is an excellent source for power.

Diver: I can do a double somersault from the top into this waterfall. It will be thrilling.

Owner of water plant: I can make so much money bottling the water from this fall. Costs for ozonisation apart, I can make a hefty profit.

Dhobi: If only I could wash my clothes here! Plenty of water here can increase my customers. I think I can even start my own laundry.

The waterfall remains one and the same but the perception changes according to the person, his profession, his wavelength of thinking.

Now, if there is only one person and if he begins to have multitude of thoughts and perceptions on the same object, what will happen? A man looking at the waterfall may suddenly admire its beauty, may start estimating its depth, calculate its potential capacity, get fearful of its cascade and so on! If these thoughts or perceptions take a regular, consolidated form he may become a poet, a scientist or a painter, channelising his ideas and thought perceptions into a constructive purpose. If he merges all his thoughts into a single concept (here it is a waterfall) he begins to reach a state of serenity. If he concentrates or focuses he attains a 'meditative' state and if he goes one step further and takes an objective look of himself, he completes his thought reflection and sublimes to a very high state of mind.

When all these are aligned in the same wavelength, you can experience a high level of realisation. This is the ultimate goal of meditation. However, the seeker of wordly things needs to unify and merge all his thoughts, align them on the same wavelength and this gives him enough mental strength to achieve his goals.

It is very difficult to align your thoughts on a single wavelength. Thoughts are like myriad branches of a tree and its very complex sub-branches. But the trunk of the tree holds all the branches and sub-branches in unity. Similarly, sustained efforts consisting of meditation and breath control can hold your thoughts in unison.

When a stone is thrown into a pond you can see the troughs and crests developing in the water. In a sea without any such intrusion the waves rise and fall. This is because of the breeze. A breeze elevates and depresses the waves. If the breeze stops the waves also calm down. Similarly, thought waves in our mind can be controlled by breath control.

Breeze control — calms sea waves

Breath control — calms thought waves

Broadcasting from a radio station is done on a regular single wave length. Similarly, thoughts in our mind can be merged into a single wavelength. Breath control, meditation help in such a merger. When we fine tune a radio, the needle stands at a single station and the reception becomes clear; similarly, thoughts are to be fine tuned on a single wavelength. Such fine tuning leads to a calm mind; calm thoughts promote calm actions. Calm actions can always lead to correct decisions!

****

9

Self-control

Tame Your Mind

Breath control leads to self-control. This alone makes you control your actions. If there is no breath control and subsequent self-control, situations, actions and fate begin to control you. We have already understood that meditation and breath control ensue a calm composed mind and this in turn ensures motivation and success. To tame your mind, tame your breath. There should be no hard, strict taming of mind. It should be a very lenient, easy going, permissive taming. Anything tamed or controlled with an authoritarian, hard, harsh method will result in an. Otherwise there will be a rebellious' outburst (resistance comes.) The mind tuns into a 'rebel' if tried to control by harsh, strict, rigorous, stern, tough means. The mind turn

➔ Taming the mind is like taming the bull.
➔ Try to be lenient + skilful in taming the mind.

submissive if controlled by simple tactics. Imagine a bull to be controlled by a matador. If he is very harsh in his fighting the bull resists. On the other hand, if he fights with a little permissive nature, the bull gets tamed. Imagine a bull fighter and a small boy both on their mission to control a bull. The matador fights, fights and finally gets killed. If the boy is going to adopt an attitude of leniency and keeps feeding the bull with grass, over a period of time the bull will turn submissive to the boy's caring nature and gets tamed. The mind is like a monkey that jumps from one tree to the other without any repose. It is restless. There is no point in controlling or taming a restless naughty monkey after it has committed a mischief. Wisdom lies in taming and controlling its naughty, disobedient nature before a mischief is committed. The mind also needs a similar treatment. It should be tamed and subdued before it turns wicked.

→ Mind is like a monkey forever restless.
→ It should be tamed before it turns wicked.
→ Prevention is better than cure.

Endearing Terms and Conditions

For every deal or agreement to be successful you must agree on mutually agreeable, amiable terms. When two parties are involved in a deal or agreement both the parties must agree on points which are endearing; it must be mutual. Only then the deal is amicable. Similarly, to tame the mind you must keep the 'interests of the mind' in the 'the tame deal'. Techniques which endear the mind must be used. There must be some expertise or knack in terms and conditions used to tame the mind. The most important point to remember is to keep the mind unaware of the fact that it is being tamed, else to the mind will rebel and revolt against its taming.

Tame the mind on its terms and conditions. Once you start

it, the mind begins to respond amicably to the 'get tamed deal'. Each and every mind is unique. Some minds are artistic where art, music, poetry, scenery, etc., endear to this kind of mind.

Some minds are rational: They need reason, logic and a basis for everything.

Some minds are calculating: Forever these minds assess, estimate, evaluate and compute.

Some minds are corporate: They seem to have only three features: business, rofit-loss, success.

Some minds are egoistic, some are full of compassion, some are extremely insensitive... and so on. Learn to endear the mind to its likes and avoid its dislikes. Make a list of all your likes. Let the mind wander, drift, the way it wants to, don't control it. Let the mind roam, stray and rove.

Even a ruffian becomes humble on seeing his sweetheart. He becomes submissive, obedient and meek by her sweet words, smile and charm. His attraction for her humbles him. Similarly, even a hard mind becomes malleable when things endearing to it are supplied.

Breath control, meditation, endearing things—all these tame a mind. Using lenient techniques integrates the mind.

The mind should get tamed on its own. It should be an unconditional surrender for the mind. It should yield on its own.

One has to help, assist and lend a hand in controlling the mind. One need not dictate. The individual must cooperate; accommodate all the whims and fancies of the mind. Finally the mind gets tamed. The effort is worth it.

The Relevance of the Bhagavad Gita in Life

Man today wants success, achievement and pleasures in large quantities. He also wants peace of mind. He himself is to be blamed, if there is a disturbance in his mind.

He has created an environment conducive to restlessness, 'neck to neck' 'retrace' competition, dissatisfaction, and if he expects peace and success in this environment, it is like keeping the hand in fire and expecting not to be burnt. He is confused and perplexed.

The *Bhagavad Gita* comes to his rescue. It gives inner strength to withstand the stress (both within and without). The *Gita's* advocacy of sublimating greed and sharing the good things of life with others helps us in our survival in this dog-eating-dog world of competition and rivalry. If there is tension in the field of action or duties the *Gita* comes to our help—teaching the modus operandi. *The Bhagavad Gita* motivates us to perform our duties and actions with zeal and zest without getting perturbed by results and consequences.

In foreign countries you have a GPS (ground positioning system) in cars and other vehicles which help you in navigation. If you get lost in your course or way from the starting point to the finishing point the GPS corrects you. It tells the correct route, correct turn and correct signal. The journey thus is in the correct direction, track and path. Similarly the *Bhagavad Gita* serves as a LPS (life positioning system), helps the 'directionality challenged' individuals and show them the correct way, the correct 'U turns' to be taken to do the right actions and the wrong 'U turns' to be avoided (to stay away from wrong actions). Life

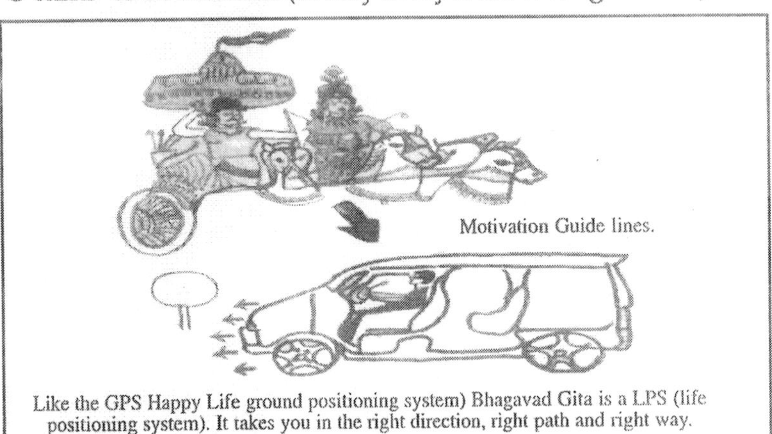

Like the GPS Happy Life ground positioning system) Bhagavad Gita is a LPS (life positioning system). It takes you in the right direction, right path and right way.

today is more complicated and there are greater choices. The *Bhagavad Gita* motivates you to make the right choice and take the right path towards your goal.

****

10
Get Motivated

The Five Ducts

We have spoken a lot about things on mind, its nature, its control, etc. What exactly is this mind? Intellect, intelligence, reason, sense, understanding — all these are the dictionary definitions of mind. Is mind only the brain? Has it got any connection to a person's emotions or innermost thoughts? Is it not the truth, that heart and mind function in some kind of agreement. Heart searching (examination of one's own feelings and motives) and heart warming (emotionally moving and encouraging) concepts are also related to the mind. When we call somebody for a heart-to-heart talk, isn't mind involved there? When somebody breaks someone's heart and causes grief the mind also comes into play.

Our brain has a lot of recorded data. It has past experiences, present happenings all stored in it. It can recall old incidents, compare them with new experiences and can analyse them. The heart supplies blood to the brain. The oxygen for the brain and the blood comes from our breathing. So a combination of heart, feelings and reason, emotions and intellect, all contribute to the state of one's mind.

Mind is nothing but various recorded data— past, present, etc. When we use the term 'brain death' we mean that the functions of the brain are dead. The brain exists anatomically even after death but its function is gone, the 'mind' is gone. Intellect, reason, sense, understanding all are gone. The mind is a factory which can survive if the raw materials (recorded data), workers (heart, 'life'), are all available in a fine condition. As long as this factory functions there is productivity. If it turns sick only a shut down is possible. The mind can make or break a person. It can either convert its recorded 'data' into effective solutions or it can project its recorded data as problems and complicated questions.

Have you seen the small ducts or canals dug out to canalise rain water into the collection areas — like ponds, lakes and other water catchment areas? If there are no rains and the dry catchment are areas neglected mud, dirt and filth get accumulated in these ducts and block them. If there are rains, instead of retrograde flow the clogged ducts/canals cause a retrograde regurgitation.

Nature has dug five canals or ducts into our minds. They are the five special senses (sense organs). The sensory information from eyes, ears, nose, skin and mouth flow into the mind. These five organs serve as ducts through which information are channelised into the mind. If the mind gets clogged, there is blockage in these ducts. All the sensory information, instead of flowing into the mind, start regurgitating out via these ducts. Valuable information of vision, auditory, tactile, taste and olfaction which should flow in via these ducts into the mind (and make it work inspiringly to motivate the person) flow out due to the block. What causes the mind to dry up? What causes the block in these sensory ducts? Pleasure seeking nature! We all want to do things which give us pleasure. We dont want anything that is painful or difficult. Due to the fear of having to encounter anything painful or difficult we don't welcome anything that is new or strange to our nature. We end up doing some futile pleasure-giving exercises again and again.

We grow up in life from an infant to a toddler, adolescent, adult, middle age, old age. All this growth is in our chronological

age, appearence, mental maturity, attitude but the basic nature remains the same. The basis for all our actions, whether driving a toy car as a child, driving a luxury car as an adult or driving a sports car as a formula race participant is pleasure seeking. Just by changing the nature of the car according to our age we have not changed our nature. This pleasure-seeking nature prevents our growth, and retards us to a juvenile, personality. One must grow up in the true sense.

Give a Red Carpet Welcome to Problems

The mind always develops an aversion towards difficulties, problems and complications. But you must realise that the maxim "No pain-no gain" holds good. There cannot be any achievement, success and accolades unless there are problems, pain, challenges and setbacks. You must condition your mind to accept pain as well as pleasure. You must admonish your pleasure-seeking mind to grow up, become more mature. Come out unscathed even in the most agonising of situations with an easy attitude towards pain. All these make a person honourable.

Learn to welcome problems, challenges and hurdles on the way to your success. They are not enemies, they are friends in disguise. If there are no problems, no pains and no hurdles, life

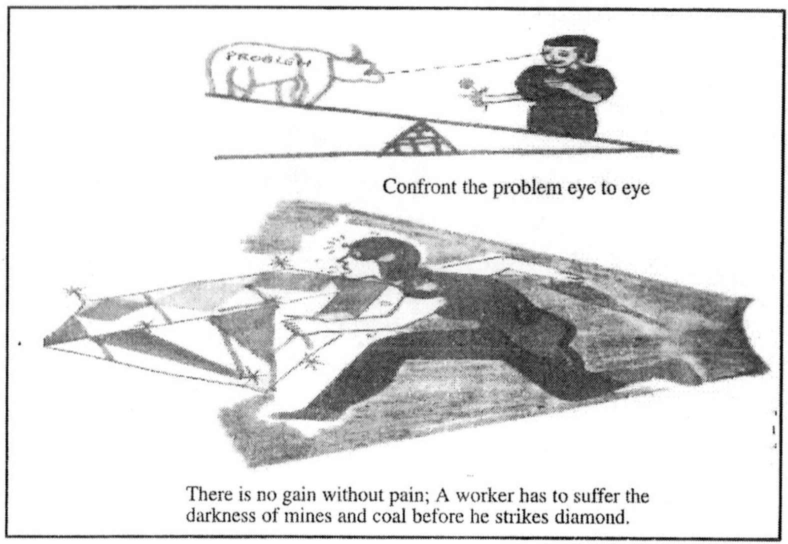

Confront the problem eye to eye

There is no gain without pain; A worker has to suffer the darkness of mines and coal before he strikes diamond.

becomes mundane, banal. Tough situations and problems don't last but if you can't handle them, welcome them. Learn to endure problems; next fight them; then come out with flying colours. Learn to adjust and adopt.

Problems and pains thrive on our immature attitudes. Don't let them have an upper hand!

Take the example of Lord Rama in the *Ramayana*. He was an ideal person in every aspect but problems didn't elude him. His father Dasharatha wanted to crown him the king whereas his stepmother Kaikeyi asked him to go to the forest for 14 years! His problems started here. In the forest Sita, his beloved wife, was abducted by Ravana. Next came the war. Even after winning back his wife and killing Ravana he couldn't rest in place. *Agnipariksha* of Sita, Sita's exile to the forest... Rama had to face so many problems and testing situations. Yet he accepted all of them gracefully and fought with grit and determination.

Even a saint is not devoid of problems and pains. He has to control his senses, conquer anger and lust, maintain an equilibrium of mind all the 24 hours, accept insults and honour with the same poise, and has to seek the Absolute in having to manage so many things he encounters so many problems and pains. Yet a true saint comes out unscathed.

If you can't tackle problems and pains in life, life itself may turn into a problem or a pain. How to tackle a problem? There are four options.

1. To consider it as a challenge. You can develop the mentality of 'let me' 'fight it out' and prove your strength.
2. To be practical and pragmatic. You can develop the mentality of 'A problem is a problem. It is there and I have to find a solution.' No cribbing and complaining attitude.
3. Comparison and consolation technique. 'I have this problem, but even he has it. His problem is severe, mine is not so bad after all. I am in a better position than he is.'
4. To develop a cool attitude. 'It's not a problem at all. Have a cold shoulder attitude towards the problem. This does not mean you avoid the problem; it means you have the upper hand, not the problem!

Running away from the problem will not help. It will make the situation more complex. You should have enough knowledge that problems can't harass you unless you want to get harassed. Develop the fighting spirit. Confront the problems. Strive to overcome them. Develop the 'awareness' that problems cannot trap you, your success, your achievements. Plan a struggle against all problems which may strike you. Face them boldly and they will vanish!

Fit for nothing' useless, unproductive— these terms are often applied to many individuals. Almost everybody gets labelled with these 'titles' sometime in life. Many people fall a prey to such insults and develop a mental handicap. They lose their a selfesteem. Often these words are applied to someone without thinking. Without realising the true potential of the person, such words are used to taunt him. These words are meant to mock, torment and tease your psyche. One should not take these words very seriously. Most of the popular figures of today have reached their present status ignoring such comments which were heaped on them in their struggling days.

You must be prepared to face criticism from others. What kind of reputation you have in your circle of friends, relatives, boss and subordinates is important. Nobody can judge you, your talents, your capacity better than 'you' yourself. Dont blindly rely on the judgement or opinion of others. You cannot bank on their review or criticism completely counting on somebody else's assessment of your worth. Only you know your true worth. Character assassination, devaluation of merit, underestimation of talents and worth, can all lead to annihilation of self-esteem, shattered self-confidence and destruction of motivation. Some people take the negative criticism, cynical and snide remarks and sceptical brickbats thrown at them too seriously, and this leads to 'psychological scars' in their psyche and paralyses them from taking any constructive step towards achievement of their goals. They become mentally handicapped, lose their enthusiasm and end up being lame ducks.

It is important that you listen to the opinions and views offered by others. This broadens your outlook and helps you in self-improvement. Constructive criticism is to be welcomed. Too much importance given to other people's views can cripple you psychologically. Function independently. Limit everybody's criticism to a point. Draw a boundary beyond which their criticism should not matter to you.

A person who is well versed in music may not know anything about cooking, and an exceptionally good cook may not know the ABC of music. Each person has knowledge pertaining to a field and he cannot pass judgments on others' particular area of specialisation. Restrict your views to your knowledge and avoid speaking about things you are ignorant about.

Be Happy

A student who wants to know what questions which will appear in his exams the next day or an expectant mother who wants to know the sex of the child in her womb lose the fun, charm and thrill of anticipation. Emotions aroused by something sudden or unexpected is great. You should not lose the element of surprise. The same thing applies to 'life'. Life does not offer readymade answers for your already prepared questions. Questions and answers change (like the course of a roller coaster ride) in life every minute.

You have to become self-sufficient, self-reliant. You have to find answers for the various questions that crop up all by yourself. This is true self-confidence. The capacity of mind is infinite. You must explore it to the maximum. You must broaden your horizon. As you do it, the magnitude of your talents, happiness, achievement increases. At the same time, your

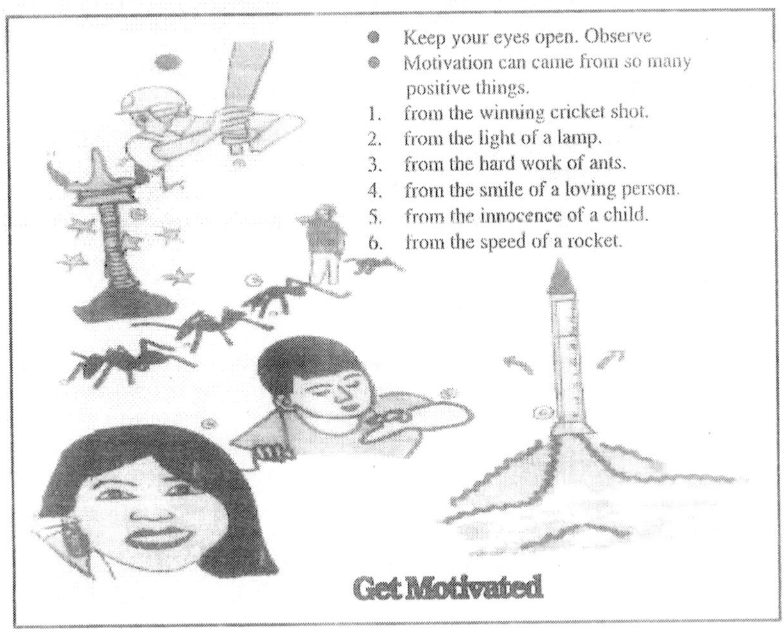

problems, pains and worries also increase in magnitude. You must develop the mental strength to tackle all of them.

Thoughts occupy the mind. Hence keep your mind in control. For this you have to practise breath control and meditation. Belief in God or a supreme force gives a lot of strength and support.

Ignore small hurdles, problems, pains which try to affect your progress. Try to use your negativities or defects to your advantage. They become a valuable investment if properly projected.

Get Motivated

1. Try to imbibe the winning qualities of a popular person.
2. Derive the motivation from the right kind of people.
3. A person with inspiring qualities should motivate you. He should be able to teach you the values and priorities of life.
4. Don't get motivate simply for the reason that a person is famous or popular. He must have substantial worth to motivate you.

Examples:

i. The compassion, magnanimity and selfless dedication of Mother Teresa.

ii. The musical talent, devotion, benevolence of M.S. Subbalakshmi.

iii. The intelligence, scientific knowledge, acumen and humility of Abdul Kalam.

iv. Hard work, charisma, versatility and acting talents of Shah Rukh Khan.

v. Grit, sportsmanhip, skill, efforts and magnanimity of Sachin Tendulkar.

6. Courage, expertise, competence, proficiency of Sania Mirza.

7. 'Business with a purpose', 'profits for charity' acts of Sudha Murthy.
8. Business acumen, 'success is my goal' attitude of Azim Premji.

Welcome constructive suggestions but avoid cynical and biased opinions. Observe the winning qualities in successful people. Get motivated by their special nature. Avoid defenceless, helpless, powerless, weak tendencies trying to surface in your mind. They can debilitate and incapacitate you. Instead of cribbing over what you don't have, concentrate on what you have, what you want to achieve. Somebody asks you the question, 'Are you a success?, Your answer should never be negative. If you think you have achieved what you wanted, say, "Yes". If you think you have not yet achieved, say, "Not yet."

Life is a festival, celebrate it.

Life is a magic, make use of it.

You cannot achieve anything by tension, worry and haste. Success achieved by short cuts and crooked means don't last. Adopt a relaxed, calm, serene attitude. Combine this with ef-

"Life is festival Celebrate it (Osho)..

"Life is a festival: celebrate it." (Osho)

forts, hard work, straightforward means and long-lasting success is sure to come. Cultivate happiness and dreams in your mind. Whether you have achieved what you aimed for or not imprint the victorious attitude in your mind; this ensures victory. You become what you think, in other words, what you think, happens, says our religious texts: *Yath Bavain Tat Bavatim:* "Think you have won and you will!"

****

Part II

PATHS TO SUCCESS

11

Motivating Concepts from the *Bhagavad Gita*

Though all the chapters of the *Bhagavad Gita* are inspiring, illuminating and motivating, certain chapters are relevant when it comes to dealing with modern day life. In chapter 5 Krishna talks about renunciation. Renunciation does not mean giving up but moving up. Renunciation does not mean giving up enjoyment it means taking up a higher enjoyment, for example, a child playing with a toy.

As it grows up it stops playing with a toy and takes up a higher enjoyment, say, a computer, but adults in majority do not move up. When they are advised to take up a higher enjoyment (or higher cause) they misunderstand. It is a lateral movement from, say, a cheap car to a costly car, from buying gold necklace to a diamond necklace; an ordinary TV to home

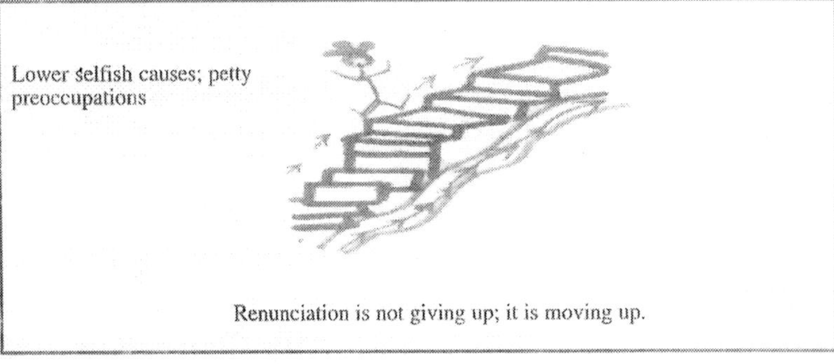

Renunciation is not giving up; it is moving up.

theatre. This is not a higher cause. Renunciation must be a vertical movement from a thing giving lower quantum of joy to a thing which gives higher quantum of joy. For example: Instead of being selfish, be selfless.

Instead of taking, try giving.

Enjoyment must be at all levels:

Spiritual
Intellectual) As one moves up, the
Emotional) quantum of joy increases.
Physical)

Look at things which give you joy from a different perspective and it may appear insane. Example:
You are happy doing an IIT or IIM course. It seems to be the be-all and end-all of your life. Now look at it from a different the view — the rat, race, the neck-to-neck competition, long tiring hours of study. It appears not so great.

Renunciation is not dispossession but all possession

- Lord Krishna himself enjoyed everything but established himself in higher concept of Atmān.
- Renuncition is having possessions but enjoying it with a dispossessive manner this gives real motivation!

Capacity Utilisation

This concept must be remembered when you talk about renunciation. You utilises only 1 per cent of capacity. In renunciation move from a not so great action to a great action. Explore this to the full capacity.

Renunciation = Capacity utilisation. This is from using

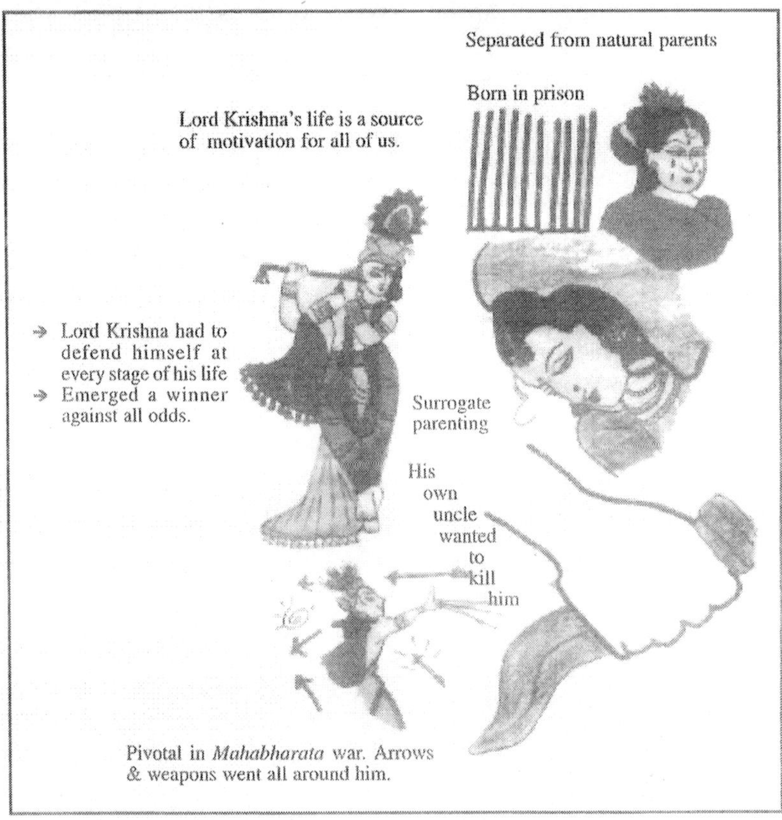

10 per cent of your capacity to using 50 per cent renunciation or even 90 per cent of capacity and potential.

When you are indulging in ordinary pleasures you are using less capacity. When you move to higher pleasures you use more of your capacity. In doing this you remove the 'blinkers' which you had put on your eyes–blinkers of ignorance, blinkers of pleasure in ordinary things, blinkers of gratification derived from cheap, mundane things. In chapter V of *the Bhagavad Gita* Lord Krishna gives a lot of information on the true meaning of renunciation.

Renunciation is not dispossession, but all possession. Lord Krishna himself enjoyed everything but established himself as the higher concept of Atman. Renunciation is having possessions but enjoying it with a dispossessive manner. This gives real motivation!

Renunciation is not life denying but life enabling. Renunciation is not giving up actions but giving up impediments to action (impediments refer to desire, ego). Here your should learn that real motivation comes from best moments of life. The best moments of life comes from being selfless. When you are self-centred you don't gain anything. When you forget yourself, think not of yourself, think of someone else, and you feel selfless emotions. This gives the best moment in your life and motivates you towards higher things.

In verse 12 of chapter V, Krishna talks about 'Yukta': One who gets ultimate peace because of foresaking the fruit of actions. He also talks about 'Ayukta': One who is bound by attachments, desire. There is bondage (no freedom).

There Lord Krishna motivates us to forsake the fruit of actions and attain peace, otherwise, he says, we will be in bondage. If you are obsessed with the fruit of actions (Ayukta) you are bound to suffer. The past affects you —so you are less focused on the present. Fear of the future affects you, worries you and hence you cannot work properly in the present.

The lesson we are taught here is: the body gets affected by everything, so don't identify yourself with the body which has limitations. Identify yourself with your mind.

It is a known fact that we are all_intellectually bound. We follow what the intellect of others dictate. Spiritually also there is bondage and some kind of surveillance. You must give up this obsession of the fruit of actions.

In verse 13 of chapter V, Krishna says that once a person mentally, not physically, renounces his fruit of actions, there is a blissful state.

Mind Body → perfect blissful state

↓ ↓

at peace acting

This motivates us to become self-controlled and attain a blissful state.

The mind at peace gives intellectual clarity. The body in dynamic action gives equanimity.

Lord Krishna himself is a classic example of mental equilibrium and dynamic actions. His dynamic actions known as his *leelas.*

Lord Krishna's life is very motivating. He suffers so much but never shows a trace of distress. The word perturb is not in his dictionary.

1. He is born in a prison.
2. He is away from his natural parents.
3. Surrogate parenting is his destiny.
4. His own uncle wants to kill him.
5. He has to defend himself at every stage of his life
6. Pivotal in *Mahabharata* war: though he has no direct role in the war he is the charioteer, with arrows flying all around him.

In spite of all this Lord Krishna emerged as a force to reckon

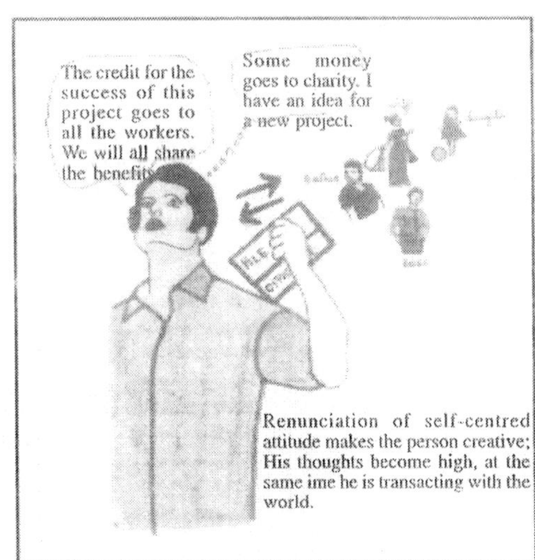

Renunciation of self-centred attitude makes the person creative; His thoughts become high, at the same ime he is transacting with the world.

with. He motivated Arjuna (who represents all of us—ever confused, distressed and undeciding). Krishna's very life is a lesson to all of us. 'Act but don't get bound to your actions' is the essence of his teachings. In verse 13, chapter V, he asks everyone to get into a state of mental silence and attain a blissful state.

In verse 14, chapter V, he Krishna separates a person and his qualities. He says, "Nature prompts one to do actions." A person may be prompted to do bad things in spite of being good. Krishna cautions us to retain objectivity in viewing people. This 'Management Mantra' followed in financial and marketing departments of huge enterprises keeps many relationships (boss-junior, junior-junior, junior-client; boss- client) intact.

It is important to know certain motivating points that Krishna illuminates here. He talks a lot about renunciation in this chapter. He says renunciation must be of trivial preoccupations which only pose a hindrance. One should renounce negative thinking. Renunciation as implied by him as moving up; choosing higher things. When the mind seeks higher things it stabilises a person. For example, one can trip over pebbles and stones but one cannot trip over mountains. When you renounces small petty preoccupations you have time and energy for 'great' things. Imagine a garage littered with junk. If you can't remove this and clean the garage your expensive car will be constantly exposed to the hot sun and heavy rains. So you need to clean the garage. The same thing applies to the concept of renunciation. Get rid of mental 'wastes' and accommodate refined, stimulating entites. Renunciation in a nutshell is intelligent waste management.

Lord Krishna stresses the need to forsake one's self-centred attitude. This brings about happiness and plenty of energy. Take the example of a baby. It is a bundle of energy, plays continuously, and is a source of unlimited action because it has no thought of the 'self'. You can function in three ways.

1. You can imitate somebody else's great action—recollective.
2. You can replicate his own great action—recreative.
3. You can create new concepts; crystallise—creative.

The creative mode is greater than the recreative mode which is greater than the recollective mode.

Renunciation of self-centred attitude makes a person creative This concept of Krishna is extremely motivating. We can be alone or in the company of others. We may seek solitude or a gathering. What is important is where our mind lies. It is so important what you seek, but it is important to keep your mind in higher thoughts, in equilibrium. Renunciation keeps your mind in a superior state.

This correct interpretation of the word 'renunciation' is important. Lord Krishna advocates renunciation for mental cleaning. Just as a sneeze brings out the foreign body from our nose, 'mental sneezing' by renunciation brings out the negativities from one's mind. Have you seen a dog getting a bath? The dog gets wet with water and then it shakes— water is everywhere except on it. Similarly all the negative thoughts must be shed in renunciation. You should try to be in an environment which generates positivity. This motivates our minds. Renunciation must also include being less involved or not being involved in others, business. You should renounce your attitude of being a self-appointed auditor of other people's characters.

What are the benefits of renunciation?

Actions done after renunciation makes a person feel rejuvenated, energised, excited, exhilarated. Success, happiness and spiritual growth begin to materialise greatly. In referring to persons who are not obsessed with the fruits of action and those who are, Krishna uses the terms Yukta and Ayukta. Yukta is 'united' and aligned, whereas Ayukta is alone, astray. Again, in chapter 5 in verses 22,23 Krishna says 'wombs of sorrow', referring to desires (enjoyments born of sense objects) and 'withstand the urge' (urges arising from passion and anger). Desire management is important in life. If a person controls his desire levels, success, happiness and spiritual growth comes to him in abundance. Socrates's words "wise man are rich" and Emerson's concept of 'Be rich by decreasing the needs and making wants few' can be recalled here. One must have wealth that selfrestraint can endure. In verses 24 and 25 of chapter 5 Krishna talks about internal *sadhana* (path of contemplation) and external *sadhana* (action path). Arjuna is confused and wants to know which should be chosen between the two paths.

For people who don't have much spiritual knowledge or 'spiritual indination action is the path. For those who have a good level of spiritual wisdom contemplation is the path.

In verse 24 Krishna talks about being happy within; this is very motivating. Happiness is not a commodity to be purchased. It is within us. You should look in, with an 'introverted' nature. *Ishavarya Upanishad* talks about three things:

The first way is the path of knowledge — Ishavarya Upanishad of action The second is the way. If a person does not follow (1) or (2) he gets into a world of ignorance, darkness and unenthusiasm. This becomes the third way or outcome.

In verse 25 'control of mind' is talked about. Here it in interesting to know what deficiency motivation is. Obsession for what one does not have is deficiency motivation and by this he misses out on all that he has. This missing out on "all that he has" is abundance awareness. To attain control of mind and happiness you should shift from deficiancy motivation to abundance awareness. By doing this shifting you get into a pay-back mode. Pay back to God, nature or society who gave you all that you use and enjoy.

We are all unaware of our abundance. We have taken everything for granted. The sun rises daily, flowers bloom, fruits ripen, birds sing, moon and stars shine— all this happen with clocklike precision. We get so many things we want, at the right place, the right time starting from our birth. We must become aware of all these gracious attributes. What you do not have you do not need. This may be nature's authority. If you don't have something, accept it that you don't need it and hence nature has kept it away from you. Charity should motivate all of us. We should all share our surplus with others.

In verse 26, chapter 5, Krishna says that once passion and anger are controlled one can realise the self and attain the Absolute. You should know a little about the three yogas often mentioned.

1. Karma Yoga: Do what you have to do. Here the concept of 'payback mode' should be practised.
2. Bhakti Yoga: This 'devotion' concept creates 'gratitude' for what we have.
3. Jnanayoga: Clarity of vision and knowledge. Knowledge of permanent and non-permanent doubts are dispelled.

Realisation comes from practice of the three yogas. Once the practice reaches the stage of self-control, there is also quality control. You get engaged the in well being of all other beings and finally there is liberation. The *Upanishads* mention these two achievements again and again to stress their importance.

The welfare of all beings to leads of liberation of thought and action and ultimately to the welfare of all beings. One get begins to get out of the 'Me, Mine, Myself' cocoon and stretches out. The service- oriented nature, accommodating interests and welfare of all the beings, materialises and this leads to realisation.

Verses 27 and 28 talk about meditation. In verses 27-28 Krishna mentions about senses-mind-intellect being in a restrained state. One should know that everybody has problems, impediments and challenges in their life. Success or defeat comes from one's attitude towards problems and challenges. One can attain a restrained state by following two simple techniques:

1. Accepting the fact that we were not promised a perfect, hassle free life at the time of our birth. So we cannot complain or grumble. It is of no use.
2. We must become aware of battles within us. There is a constant battle going on inside us, spirit against flesh, good thoughts against evil thoughts, logic against fantasy. This should motivate us towards 'fight it out' temperament.

Restraint does not mean a holding back from performing right actions or fighting the right battles. It means checking, controlling, curbing the desires, anger, passion which can destroy our motivation and progress. This fight-it-out spirit or temperament takes you towards realisation.

In verses 27-28 Krishna mentions about 'shutting out internal contacts' while meditating. This shutting should be mind-oriented, not physical. You should shut out external contacts, not bodily, but in mind. It should be a mental phenomenon, not anatomical.

The essence of all these discussions are:

1. Practice of three yogas decreases desires.
2. Mind by nature is restless, so it shifts during meditation. Intellect (intelligence + reason + understanding) must bring it back.
3. Breath control (balancing incoming and outgoing breath) gives self-control.
4. You should free yourself from desires as they are the root cause of fear, and anger desires leads to insecurity which leads to fear. Desires, if unfulfilled, kindles anger.
5. Consistent, constant, alert effort must be made to get hold of your goal, whether it is worldly or spiritual. In the last verse 29 of chapter 5, Krishna says, "Knowing one's atman, one gets peace, i.e. self-realisation leads to peace." Here 'knowing' is with reference to *Atman* and not Lord Krishna.

Lord Krishna asks us to realise our 'Atman' and attain peace.

In chapter 5, Krishna asks the entire human race (represented by Arjuna) to visualise the 'entity' maintaining the universe. In this verse Krishna mentions Tapas and Yagna. Intelligent conservation, redirection and recollection of energy focused on a goal is Tapas. Working for a higher cause is Yagna.

Today we are in a world of meritocracy where your merit decides what you get. The practice of Tapas and Yagna will make you get all that you aspire for.

Krishna stresses on inward looking, selfanalysis and inner

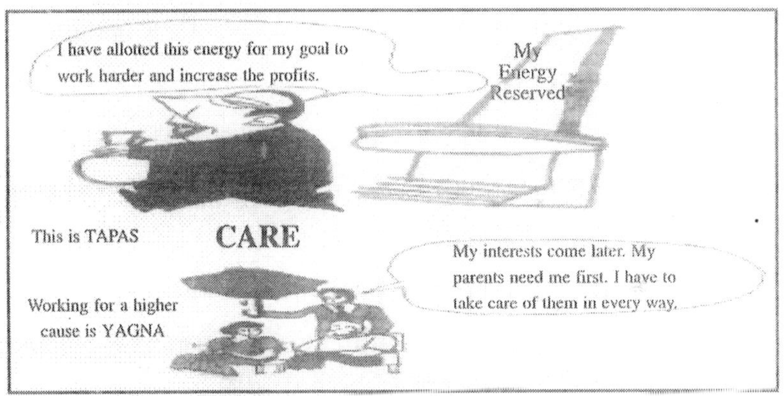

(self) study. Applying this concept to our modern life what happens with this inward looking attitude?

Outward-looking

1. Such a person is always unhappy.
2. No enthusiasm.
3. Constant thought and actions to fulfil desires leads to increased stress.
4. The good in you vanishes.

5. Burden to society.
6. Lonely in spite of friends.
7. Depends on outside things for happiness.
8. Negative frame of mind, is like a spectator inside a boxing ring getting bashed up for no reason at all.
9. In a desert of agitation and disturbance you are searching and running for a mirage called desires, its fulfilment.

Inward-looking

1. Such a person is always happy.
2. Enthusiastic, optimistic.
3. 'Introspection' leads to cheer.
4. You can spot your talents and work on your positives.
5. Asset to society.
6. Everybody becomes a friend.
7. You become a source of happiness to people around you.
8. Positive frame of mind.
9. A spectator in audience enjoying the match.
10. In a desert of agitation disturbance, you are an oasis of peace and tranquillity because of your nature.

Lord Krishna makes it clear that human beings alone can rise above agitation and visualise higher things and move up to it.

After every disaster and every challenge, human beings emerge as, better persons. Challenges, disasters sharpen your skills like an abrasive sharpening a knife.

When you face a challenge you become more skilled and aware of your determination and reach out to your goal and success.

Body control, mind control, seclusion, the mind free of desires the right intellect all are important for meditation.

****

12

Transcending Desires

We saw few concepts from chapter 5 of the *Bhagavad Gita*. Now let us turn our attention to chapter 13: 'Discrimination between nature and soul.' This chapter has certain inspiring thoughts which are sure to motivate us. It focuses on 'spirit' (mind or animating principles distinct from body; soul). This chapter in synopsis asks us to get uplifted from matter to spirit. Matter and spirit are differentiated by 'subtle intellect' in human beings.

In totality, we are spirit (*Kshetrajna*) not *Kshetra* (matter).

How can one understand this concept? Just consider a television and a viewer and a car and a driver. *Kshetra* (here) is TV and car while *Kshetrajana* (here) are viewer, driver.

Escalation from physical to higher levels (matter to spirit) bring infinite happiness. How can you achieve this? We can recollect from previous discussions that desires distort clarity of thoughts and bring unhappiness. This is because one is still at the physical level. Lord Krishna danced on the head of serpent Kalia—here the head represent desires, Krishna dancing on its head represents symbolically suppression of desires. Once you do it, you win. This is the message. A question arising is, are desires bad? Not at all. 'Desire Management' is the need of desire assassination. One should not allow desires to manifest without the sanction of intellect, because uncontrolled desires cause problem whereas controlled desire motivate and help in progress.

One can compare uncontrolled desire to a disease and controlled desire to a vaccine.

Our Vedantic texts stress uplifting one's values from physical materialistic to higher realms—emotional, intellectual, spiritual. This implies raising the quality of desires. When the quality of desires increases (upgraded desire) stability (satisfaction) also increases.

The quantum of desires descreases automatically when one transcends the physical limitations.

One can explain the above concept as follows: Suppose a person likes sweets. He eats them; the desire is at the physical level—satisfaction. If he gives the sweets, the desire is at the emotional level.

Consider a poet or an artist. The poet is able to conceive a beautiful poem. An artist is able to paint an inspiring painting. Here desire operates at the intellectual level to create a thought. provoking-poem and to paint a true-to-life picture. All these are intellectually stimulating. In this intellectually satisfying

pursuits the fulfill ment derived is much more than in physical/ emotional levels.

Now let us consider Mahatma Gandhi. His desire was linked to the spiritual level. Here the satisfaction derived is maximum.

So the message of *the Bhagavad Gita* is to abstain from uncontrolled desires. In verse 28 of chapter 13 Lord Krishna uses the word 'samam'. *Samam* refers to internal understanding and a state of peace within. Here Lord Krishna asks everybody to adopt an impartial view while evaluating others. You should perceive goodness in others and to do it you have to be good yourself. This is an important management mantra. First develop the quality (you want to see in others) in you and then look for it in others. Remember only a good person can perceive goodness in others. If one is bad one can see only evil in others. *Othello,* a play of Shakespeare, is to be recollected here. The husband is suspicious of his wife. Everything she does is misconstrued by him. Lord Krishna asks one to become that which have wants in others. In chapter 13, verse 28, the word 'Samam' has a lot of meaning. The 'superior principle dwels in all beings equally; in other words all beings are reflections of you'. Realise this, says Krishna. A realised person's perception will be "All beings are reflections of me." This perception motivates one tremendously.

Start seeing everybody as reflections of your own self. Develop an equality in viewing others.

Lord Krishna asks every being to adopt this view of *Samam*. If you can't see everybody as reflections of your own self you feel threatened, vulnerable, aggressive and insecure. If this continues, you destroy yourself. If, on the other hand, you can see others as your reflections, you go to higher goal and realisation. You must first accept the fact that you have a wrong perception and that your must change it. Only a slow and detailed perception can enlighten you.

In verse 30 Krishna's message to human beings is 'stop being body centric. Go to higher levels of mind, intellect. Then become the true seer, otherwise you remain blind'.

In verse 31, chapter 13 Krishna talks about the one true enlivening substratum which acts as the energising force that allows actions to take place. One should understand this. You must understand that all beings converge into that energising force and all diverge again from it.

The *Bhagavad Gita's* main message to the entire mankind is: "Human existence is to conceive something higher, subtler, but real."

Lord Krishna In the *Bhagavad Gita* implies 'Nothing comes to you by chasing or running behind it. stop! Take a U turn away from it and the thing comes flying to you automatically.

Scientists and science consider only material and matter. They want to restrict their horizon to the obvious. But one should accept the fact that nothing is complete or whole with the obvious. The philosophy and spiritual sciences say 'spirit' makes this entire universe function. Just as you cannot solve a maths problem without sufficient data, you cannot solve your problems without the data called 'Spirit.' A spiritually 'blind' person finds your world a boring, bleak and grey place whereas a spiritual person finds the world to be magnificent and vibrantt. You should have motivation to perceive beyond the obvious. If you go beyond this, you will conclude that spiritually seen life is beautiful, full of grandeur. You become aware of this perfectly well designed universe. You begin to ask, 'Who is the architect of this universe?' This curiosity takes you to higher levels.

You should first focus on what is beyond the obvious. This gives clarity of thoughts.

Everythings falls into place (even in wordly life) Once a person begins to focus on 'permanent concepts' he stops worrying about changes in trascient aspects. When he aligns with the 'spirit' then he enjoys fluctuations of body, mind, intellect. He begins to enjoy health and ill health with the same ease. If a person is going to be obsessed with the 'body', ill health stresses him mentally and he cannot recover. The *Vedanta* says, 'healthy mind→healthy body.' You must realise that injuries of the mind like grief and sorrow, get healed by nature's own ways.

Chapter 13 tells us to see beyond the obvious. When this is done you learn to differentiate between *Kshetra* and *Kshetraja* (Field → Knower of field).

****

13

Align with Your 'Self'

The *Bhagavad Gita in* 101 verses gives you knowledge in all it words, all its lines. Each word and line has profound implications. Verse 32 of chapter 13 asks man to align with the *Atman* (or spirit). If this is done he is secure.

Krishna asks one to 'get free' by identifying and aligning with the spirit or atman—the timeless, pure, imperishable, supreme entity. It never diminishes, says Krishna.

This can be explained by following the concept of gold got from a gold mine. It can be made into sheets of gold, into an ornament, or melted liquid gold.

In all the three ways gold proper remains the same, whether in the form of a sheet, an ornament or liquid. Similarly, the spirit or atman is unchanged-imperishable principle within our body (whatever be our form). Atman never becomes sad or depressed. This realisation motivates a person. The core of one's being is redemption—slight readjustment is one's perception is the need.

Again and again Lord Krishna motivates mankind to align with the atman.

Imagine an investor. If the value of his stocks increases or decreases in the share market he gains or loses. But the stockbroker, a mediator, remains unaffected. The atman is like a stockbroker unaffected. Aging, death, etc., nothing affect it. For example, electricity manifests as 'light' in a lamp, breeze in a fan, but it remains unchanged. Only the equipment manifests.

Only the body-mind-intellect function but the spirit remains the same. It is neutral and infinite. Take the example of a trained musician. He can play divine music if given a flute or sitar. An untrained person playing these instruments brings out horrible music. Take, for example, an actor playing various roles. If he has the role of a villain in real life he doesn't become bad in real life. He remains untainted his atman remains untainted. Once a person realises this— that the atman is immaculate, neutral he gets *sama darshanah:* equal vision to all beings. Gandhiji's words 'Hate the sin, not the sinner' is apt here. When you have equal vision for all, you can differentiate the deed and the person doing it.

Both the court-rooms and the board rooms need this equal

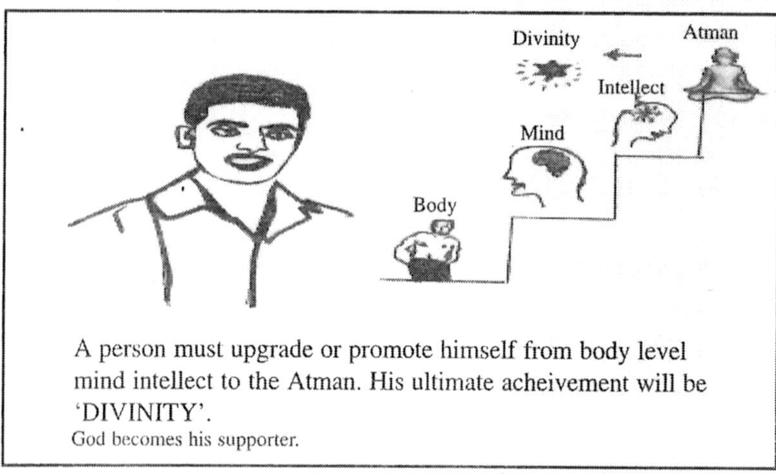

A person must upgrade or promote himself from body level mind intellect to the Atman. His ultimate acheivement will be 'DIVINITY'.
God becomes his supporter.

vision and the discrimination of deed and performer (of deed). This can remove unwanted bias, rivalry and injustice.

Verse 33 in chapter 13 says as the sun illuminates the world the soul or atman illuminates all bodies. The person who is 'aware' rejoices, basks in the light of the atman. Often we see knowledge being compared to light, and atman to sun. Imagine a room full of furniture—chairs, tables, shelves, stands, etc. If a person has to walk from one end of the room to the other end in darkness, what happens? He need not rearrange the furniture to make way for him, he needs to carry a candlelight. This will enable him to walk without tripping over furniture. Similarly, in this world one needs the light of knowledge to dispel the darkness of ignorance and walk in the room (life or world can be compared to room) without getting hit by obstacles, challenges, lifestyle demands, haves and have nots as decided by our judgement). Here one needs soul searching, awareness of soul, its worth. While being aware of this soul one also needs to do some soul bashing! Never have bad feelings, hatred, ill thoughts for anything or anybody. These things take away your strength and power to fight against evil. You lose your strength to stand for right convictions if you have negative feelings. Bask in the right knowledge, its light illuminates you. This is Krishna's message.

In the last verse (34) of chapter 13 Krishna says those who have gained wisdom by clear discrimination between matter and spirit have become aware of *Kshetra* (field) and *Kshetrajana* (Knower of the field) and must practise this wisdom. They helps them get rid of transient things and move to permanent concepts. Liberation comes to them. Liberation means being amidst matter but unaffected by it. Uuntouched yet living in matter is true liberation. This gives you the ability to conduct yourself with diginity.

Krishna says evil is within and we must fight them. He asks everyone to be calm, assertive, and to develop intellectual clarity. He cautions us to stay away from mental agitation and support goodness in every form. Atman is defined as an 'entity' list, light of light and the goal of knowledge, lodged within each individual. One should delve deep into the superficial layers of personality. Transcend the physical and get into soul searching, exploring the atman, the core of everything. This is Krishna's message.

Krishna first explains the cultivation of 21 qualities and internalisation of knowledge which culminates into wisdom. Next he asks us to look within, accept our faults, overcome them, proceed to knowing what is worthwhile and then achieve realisation. The realisation means growing from limited to infinite personality. Just as a child gives up its toys as it grows up you too must give up your petty preoccupations (pertaining to that stage). There must be exploration. Stepping out of a comfort zone to know the ultimate is important. You gain more meaningful entities by this exercise. You should be brimming with irresistable urge to explore and your goal should be realisation. In verses 20 (chapter 13) and 21 there are discussions on matter, spirit (*prakriti, purush*) at some length. What you need to know is that the atman retains all its inherent properties in spite of aberrations, modifications, distortions, all coming from body, mind, intellect.

Lord Krishna urges mankind to 'wake up' and give up the sleep of ignorance. Krishna also points out that negative experiences brings out enlightenment or a revolution. Take the example of Buddha. He saw death, an old man's plight, disease and this bought him wisdom; Mahatma Gandhi was thrown out of a train in South Africa which kindled revolutionary instincts in him. Negative experiences brings a cleansing effect, a catharsis—often making us realise what is true, positive and worth knowing.

Krishna talks about the various roles God plays. According to a man's nature a person is totally negative, evil to himself and others— God is an onlooker. If the person is less selfish, God says 'Go ahead'. He is a permitter and aids in removing

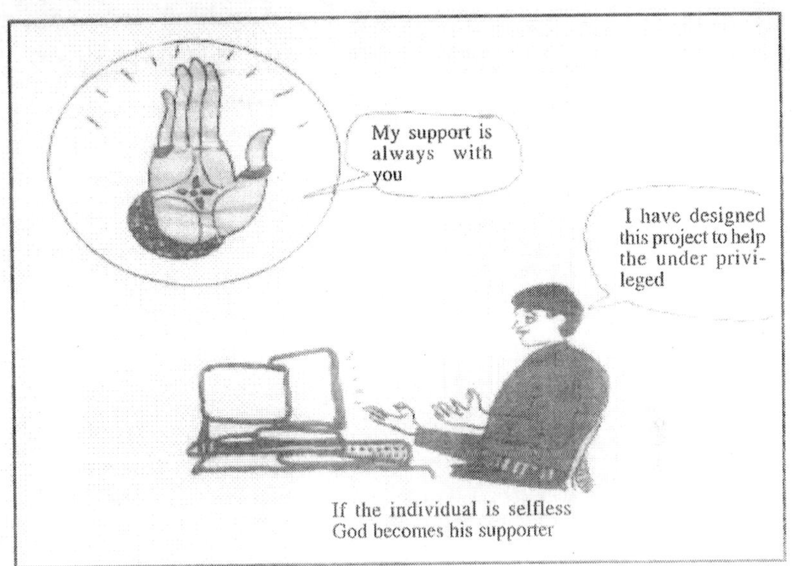

If the individual is selfless God becomes his supporter

the final trace of selfishness. If the person is self-less, God becomes a supporter.

The formula for happiness and success is keeping one's desire level at moderate levels, being selfless and assertive. You should be motivated enough to do things which are right and essential. The sense of having done what has to be done gives an immense feeling of fulfilment. Self-indulgence never gives this satiety. You should grow to higher dimensions, escalate your ideals, upgrade you thoughts. Body-mind-intellect (BMI) is a prison. You can be a 'criminal' or a 'freedom fighter' in this prison. Both these are put in jail but their actions and attitudes are totally different; a criminal has done something evil whereas a freedom fighter has done something venerable: to fight for his nation. A criminal feels suffocated in a jail whereas a freedom fighter enjoys even a prison life as an honour. You should develop a 'let go' attitude and have a 'detached' attitude + duty-bound sense. This alone can give joy. Anything done with an attached mind yields sorrow. Krishna talks of three stages:

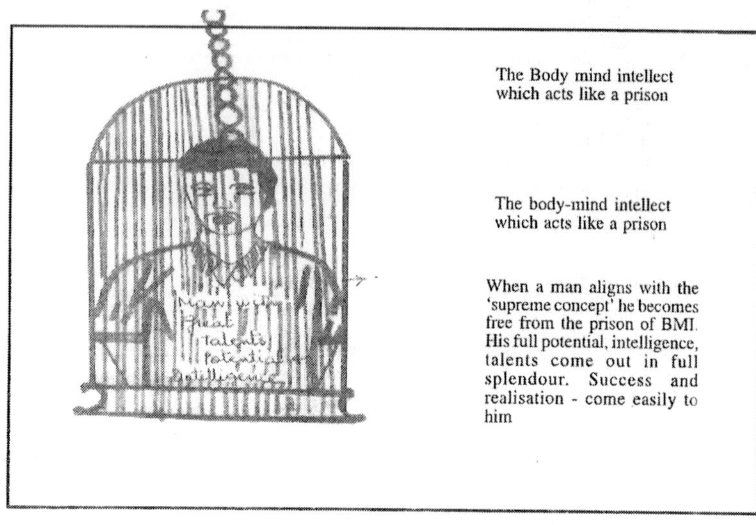

being extrovert ➔ sorrow

being introvert ➔ peace

being united ➔ infinite bliss

When you are attached and searching for happiness and satisfaction from external sources only sorrow comes; if you can upgrade to 'soul searching', 'gazing into inner yourself', introspecting', you find peace. When you are 'united' and you have 'realised', duty conscious but unattached' aims for higher things in life', you get bliss.

The *Bhagavad Gita* again and again stresses on refinement of desires. A well controlled, guided, disciplined desire alone can yield success and joy.

Desire can be categorised into two groups: Desires unscanned by intellect, desires scanned by intellect, desires unscanned by intellect leads to: anger, lust, avarice.

Any desire (wished for or acheived) must become an objective with some purpose. It should be guided and controlled by intellect.

Desires scanned by intellect becomes ambition, a goal, a mission objective.

The desire for money should not become a greed-driven selfish accumulation of wealth. It should become a service-oriented enterprise. Infosys, the computer corporate giant, is making millions but Infosys Foundation, its conception, is using the millions for service, charity and benevolence. There is nothing wrong in aspiring for a post or promotion. You can even desire to become a prime minister but it should not be for personal gains, it should be with the aim to serve. You can desire for attractive good looks but it should not be a vain, conceited exercise. There should be a purpose in that beauty; there should be an effort to become beautiful by nature, thoughts, words and deeds. Internal beauty is more important than external beauty. Robert Browning calls it 'imprisoned splendour'. This word has profound implications. You should not confine your desires, talents, potential for selfish means. It should be for the betterment of the entire human race—selfless and considerate gesture. When you are is motivated to work for others your own hidden potential comes out and you become aware of your worth!

- ➔ Aishwarya Rai (Miss World 1994) — a classic example of 'beauty with a purpose'.
- ➔ One should go beyond body.to higher planes.
- ➔ Aishwarya Rai has donated her eyes and compaigns for eye donation.
- ➔ One should stop being 'body centric' and reach for a higher cause.
- ➔ External beauty is transient, but the internal beauty—the thoughts, attitude, and nature serving a definite purpose is long lasting.

****

14

Attachment and Detachment

The separation of the three gunas has some important messages to convey. Verse 1 talks of supreme knowledge. Here it will be interesting to know that all the beings in this world are dependent on the world for their existence. Human beings alone can control this world. This is so unique. At their 'intellect' level they have this supremacy, and if a person moves to higher levels (spiritual, knowledge of atman) he can achieve even greater goals. As you move from the lower to the higher knowledge you can aim for the limitless infinite. Krishna in verse 2 of chapter 14 says, "Having anchored with knowledge" a man gets established in 'permanence' and moves away from the transient fleeting things. Once a man gets focused on the atman he moves away from 'at the scene as a subject' entity to the onlooker of the scene' entity. Once a person achieves 'union with the self', he becomes selfless, happy, and focused.

Imagine a person buying or selling a jewel from a goldsmith. When he buys a jewel, he is excited, interested in the design of the jewels, its cost, etc. When he sells the jewel, he is sad as he has to part with a precious jewel.

Now take the example of the goldsmith who buys or sells the jewel from the person. He is unaffected. He sells the jewel and buys the jewel with the same attitude. He does not have discriminition in the deal whether buying or selling. This is the 'I am not involved' mode.

Take the example of a sea. The sea is not bothered about its waves being high or low. But a person watching the waves gets excited if there are high tides and gets bored if the tides become low. So once you are involved you get affected. One must adopt this 'not involved' mode, 'I am not a part of it' attitude. This leads to a focused view. Krishna says, for happy survival one needs to have the knowledge of the atman; this alignment with the atman makes you focused and keeps you away from turmoils.

In the wordly parlance, knowledge of higher concepts helps us in creating small reserves of truth, ethics, values, etc., around us, distancing us from sorrows and disturbances. In verse 4 of chapter 14 Krishna talks about 'unity' of all beings. He recommends repeated thinking and contemplation which lead to wisdom. There are two types of knowledge in this world: (1)Knowledge pertaining to one particular field—when a person has knowledge relevant to his field of excellence he restricts his 'know-how', grasp and learning to a limited level (2) The knowledge pertaining to higher concepts-Self-Atman, Soul—makes the person 'well versed'—a highly knowledgeable, enlightened, wise person. This unconditioned knowledge (or supreme knowledge) takes the person to true realisation.

. Lord Krishna in chapter 14 classifies the nature of men as Rajas, Tamas, Sattva — the three 'gunas'.

The characteristic Principle of Tamas is ignorance

The characteristic Principle of Rajas is passion.

The characterest Principle of sattva is wisdom.

Sustained growth is not possible unless you establish yourself in Sattva. Sattva is in line with divinity, unity and totality. Sattvik thoughts (noble, unselfish thinking) vitalises a

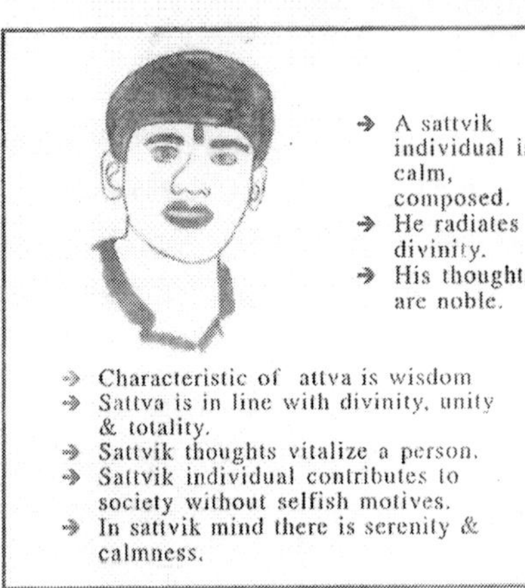

person. The Sattvik person contributes to society without selfish motives.

Every man has Sattva, Tamas, Rajas qualities in him but in different proportions. The Sattvik nature comes out predominantly in the early morning hours before the sun rises. Sunrise to sunset— Rajas manifests and after sunset Tamas manifests. Our ancient scriptures say that a person must choose his vocation or occupation in line with his gunas. What should be the aim of a man who wants to improve his character, disposition, temperament and essential qualities? He should eqradicate Tamas refine, Rajas, and establish and Sattva.

Sattva surfaces in mind in the predawn period and you must utilise this time adequately. The *Bhagavad Gita* and *Vedanta* stress on human perfection. Both say that human beings are already perfect but are covered by *gunas*. This can be compared to a floodlight covered by a blanket. Once this blanket is removed the light shines brightly.

1. Tamas Mode — light covered by a blanket—inertia, can't act.
2. Rajas Mode — There is action but desires, egos, pollute the mind and cause resistance or blocks. Rajas mode can be compared to a light covered by a thin sheet not a thick blanket.
3. Sattvik — This nature is 'perfection' in every aspect

   There is serenity in mind.

Sattva helps in shaping the desires, ego

Sattva is uncovered bright light.

There is effortless excellence Krishna says there is 'Divinity' within each individual but the coverings of *Gunas* keep it sealed. Here we should recall what Michael Angelo said, "Inside every block of wood or stone there is a beautiful statue; the sculptor merely removes the excess material.'

Similarly, if we can shape our *gunas*, we can become superior. Sattva is unknown and remains unexplored in most of the individuals. You should realise its worth and develop it. If you do not develop the Sattvik nature and enhance your Sattva, Tamas and Rajas predominate and take over. Tamas must be conquered by developing a 'self-punishment' technique. Rajas needs refinement. You can give yourself a high ideal this increases your dynamism, energy. Selfishness, enervates a person. Unselfish ideal, energises unselfish actions even if not successful it gives a sense of fulfilment and satisfaction.

Just as there is a' Microsoft for dummies for computer illiterates the *Vedanta* is for Tamas-Rajas dominated Sattvik illiterates.

Sattvik mentality: healthy mind, healthy body, right, actions
Rajas/Tamas mentality: ill mind, ill body, wrong actions.

For a spiritual aspirant he must of let go of Sattva. That is, he must go beyond the *gunas*. If he is going to be obsessed with Sattva and Sattvik practises he may become 'spiritually entangled' (like attachment to a guru, ashram, etc.) Hence, he must transcend Sattva also.

Whether spiritual or worldly you must be duty bound but unattached. Take the example of Fevicol. When you fix something with Fevicol it is too tightly glued and you can't take it out. On the other hand, if you use 'Stick On' this rubber, mastic adhesive fixes, mounts, holds, secures but can be easily removed by rolling over on the surface. This must be one's nature, one must be duty bound, but unattached.

In verse 7 chapter 14, Krishna says, Rajas is passion; it breeds thirst and binds to action.

With the action of Rajas mode first the feeling of emptiness comes, then passions, desires, longing, craving, thirst for something. If one gets these, it leads next to attachment to that them. This cycle goes on and on. Lord Krishna points out that the very first 'Feeling of emptiness is imaginary and a trick of Rajas. There is nothing wrong in desires and acquiring things but the right interaction is important. Most of the individuals interact with their acquired success so unintelligently that ultimately it leads to sorrow and pain.

One must develop a dispassionate or detached attitude to happiness. Rajas mode leads to craving and often prevents one from reaching one's goal as there is a clouded mind. Sattva mode, on the other hand, leads to: serenity, clear thinking, easy attainment of goal.

In verse 8 (chapter 14) Krishna elaborates on 'Tamas'—born

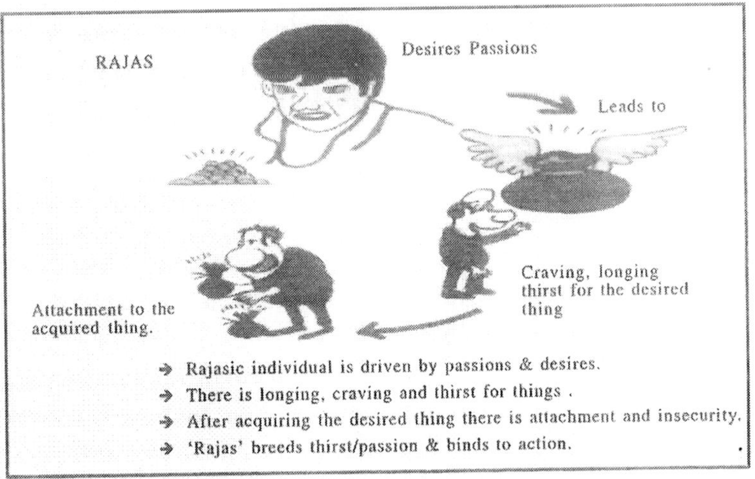

of ignorance it binds by sleep, lethargy and decreased alertness. Here it will be of use to know about 'Ignorance'.

Ignorance	Absolute	Relative
There are various questions like:		
1) One does not know he is the atman.		1) Why were we born?
2) He believes he is body-mind-happen?		2) When will death intellect.
3) He restricts himself to finitude and sorrow (whereas he is denying him self infinity and total bliss.		3) What is life. 4) Why does a baby of 4 years suffer from cancer spending nearby 50% of its life time in hospital and dies....

A person must shed his ignorance and search for 'knowledge' (in the real sense. Once a person knows about the vast knowledge he is yet to learn about his judgemental attitude. Tamas at the body level is bad but at the mind and intellect level it is worse.

Lord Krishna says, Sattva attached to bliss is like a transit halt at a pleasant place. You should not stay there permanently. Once the destination becomes clear there will be no attachment.

Here it will be interesting to know the story of an English movie which emphasizes the importance of being clear about one's destination. A man gets convicted for a crime he has not committed. He ends up in jail. But from day one his destination or aim is to finish his sentence and go out to his family—his loving wife and beautiful kids whom he adores. He has no attachment, no hatred to the jail or the prison inmates. He neither loves the kind-hearted cellmate nor does he hate the wicked prison warden. His only destination is 'Finish my term; go out

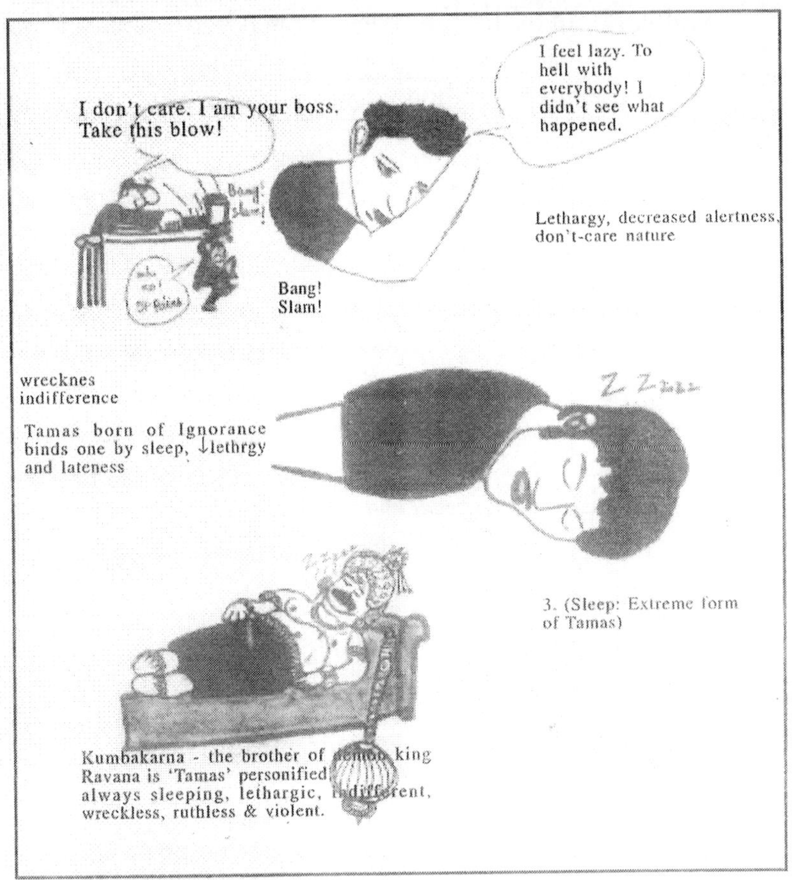

to my family.' Being a mechanic by vocation he has a good knowledge of cars. In the jail yard he finds an old, out-of-condition car. His mechanic skills come into action. To pass his leisure time, with the help of his jail mates, he begins to repair the car. He paints it, reassembles the damaged parts, oil and cleans it—makes the car brand new. But the day he plans to make it run the wicked prison warden smashes the repaired car to derive some sadistic pleasure. All the inmates are furious, but he is not at all affected by the car's deplorable state, as his goal is to finish his sentence and go out to his family. His destination is 'out of the jail—back to the family'. This attitude of clear-cut decision on destination and 'unattached' state of mind comes from 'clear thinking', full of clarity— a Sattva mode of action.

Sattva must be practised but should not become an obsession.

Rajas binds to action. As desire increases stress and attachment to actions also increase. Tamas (shrouded in knowledge) leads to heedlessness and there is reckless indifference.

In verse 11 of chapter 14 Lord Krishna talks about the radiant manifestation of Sattva. An individual who has Sattvik qualities has the following characteristics:

1. He has no conflict with anybody. Perfectly united.
2. His actions are aesthetic and attractive.
3. His actions are ethical, knowledge-guided.
4. Brilliance becomes his identity.
5. There is clear perception, insight, purity.
6. His actions are skilful, productive.
7. He is a self-governed individual (needs no policing).
8. He can 'adjust' and 'adapt' with changes in life.
9. His intellect is unbiased, unprejudiced, objective with the following: observation—insight—concept — actualisation plan.
10. His mind is pure with unselfish emotions, true love, non-attachment, operating on collective agenda (other's interest hospital matters to him, and he aligns with divine agenda (acceptance).
11. He is aware of his abundance.

In Rajas craving and greed makes a person act by deficiency

motivation. He chases desires, becomes restless, agitated—what he has, becomes irrelevant to him. Krishna implies, "Nothing comes by chasing or running after; on the other hand, if he stops chasing, the thing automatically cames to him. A Sattvik person is aware of his abundance. 'He can feel like a millionaire without a million'. His actions become an offering, thanks- giving to God.

The *Bhagavad Gita* repeatedly stresses on the importance of mental focus. Physical action comes later.

In verse 13, chapter 14, Lord Krishna says that Tamas leads to darkness. There is no concept of right things. An individual with Tamas predominating in him has an absurd life. He acquires things, enjoys them and dies.

Lord Krishna talks in detail about the three *gunas* (nature of an individual), their characterstics, their mode of action, how they dominate or remain unexplored. The three *gunas* operate through desires. Desire is like a fire, a disaster waiting to happen. It is like a beautiful flame of a lamp or candle. It is up to the guna to keep it as a flame or make it a devastating uncontrollable fire.

Just as a spark of fire can turn into an inferno, which can even burn a forest, similarly, uncontrolled desires, destruction, finish a man completely. If he has Sattva in sufficient quantities his desires remain controlled.

Sattvik qualities function as 'continuous, ceaseless, nonstop' pouring of water over the fires of desire. Sattva extinguishes hatred, negativities and desires (uncontrolled) just as water puts out a fire. Krishna states:

Sattva manifests when it overpowers Rajas and Tamas.

Rajas manifests when it overpowers Sattva and Tamas.

Tamas manifests when it overpowers Sattva and Rajas.

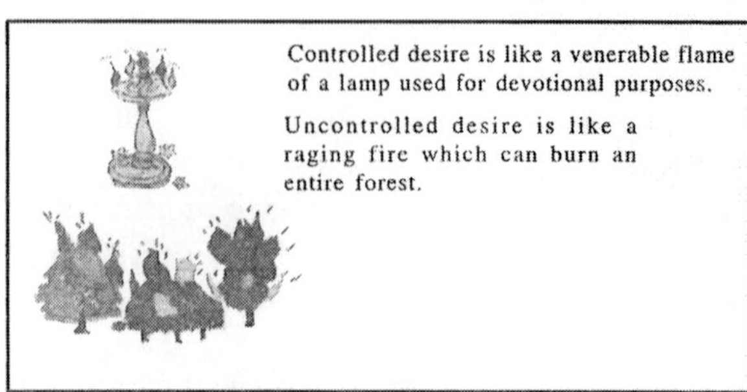

Success in worldly pursuits depends on one's Sattvik content.

Success in spiritual pursuits depends on going beyond Sattva.

In India the great country with its population of a billion people, different cultures, languages, religions, castes, creed, there is unity in diversity. This unity (spiritual unity and unity of humanity) is because of 'Sattva' in each one of us. All of us, in spite of differences, are working in tandem. This is because of Sattva and its attributes. India can become the leader of the world if only the entire Sattva in its entire population is explored and tapped.

In India, from north to south, from east to west one common item of food is eaten. This is curd (yoghurt or dahi). The bacteria lactobacillus can grow in our intestines only by the facilitation of curd. It helps in two ways. Vitamin B production–maintaining a PH which keeps normal bacterial flora intact—prevents harmful bacterial growth.

Similarly Sattva creates a PH in mind which prevents growth of negative thoughts, produces serenity and at the same time maintains a PH (state of mind) for the thoughts so to thrive.

Here one can recall our ancient Indian's daily routine. The day began in ancient times at predawn (before sunrise), so the mind was charged with positive thoughts as Sattva manifiests at this time of the day predominantly. Once the sun came up people got busy with their occupation and at night there was unwinding or relaxation in the form of prayers, devotional music and recitation of sacred texts. The Sattva, thoughts full of positive ideas and serenity which were charged in the mind early morning, was utilised throughout the day making the whole day productive.

Tamas was not entertained and Rajas was maintained at minimum levels (enough to help in hard work).

Just as we charge a call phone or emergency lamp with a charger we need to charge our body-mind-intellect with Sattvik nature. The outcome will be Sattvik actions, words and thoughts. Actions become productive, thoughts selfless and words endearing and sincere.

Imagine the routine in a gym.

First: warm up of stretching exercises, then by doing hard, sweating, workout. Finally, relaxation, unwinding.

Warm up with Sattvik mode, the whole day, can be made productive and useful with the positive thoughts, actions and words. Relax in the night with serenity and calm state of mind.

Have you been in an elevatator or a lift? It hoists or lifts something up to the level desired. The same principle applies as despicted in the *Bhagavad Gita.* If you do not want to go to the spiritual level, you can very well get down to the level of worldly things. If you do not want realisation you can restrict yourself to success. The *Bhagavad Gita* has something for everybody. It teaches you to achieve worldly pleasure, success and your goal by giving you the right guidelines to follow. If your aim is spiritual enlightenment, it *Bhagavad Gita* shows you the way for it. The principles declared by Lord Krishna can be applied for spiritual and worldly life. The can be appropriately fitted for both material success and spiritual progress.

Have you seen a supermarket? It has something to offer for every shopper. Some choose costly things, some buy cheap things; some buy a lot; some only a few; some prefer window shopping and others buy almost the entire shop. The same thing applies as the *Bhagavad Gita* expostulates. Spiritual aspirants seek the realisation. Each can pick and choose according to his taste and needs.

The *Bhagavad Gita* has motivation lessons for every class of people. The basic principles are the same. One can apply the doctrine to one's chosen target/purpose.

****

- All the beings in this world are dependent on the world for their existence
- Human beings alone can control the world. This is because of their unique intellect.

Part III
PERSONALITY DEVELOPMENT

15

The Secrets of Success

Personality developmet is important for gaining success. The development of one's personality is a challenging task. It needs hard, methodical labour, perseverance and careful attention. The outcome of a well developed personality is rewarding and no effect in this direction goes waste.

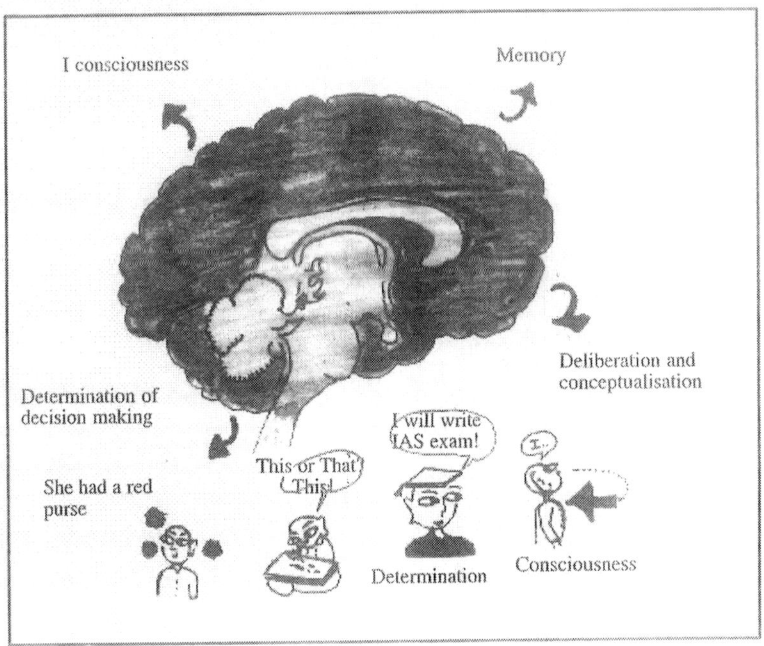

Personality is the whole nature or character of a person. Your personality is the type of person you are, which is shown by the way you behave, feel and think. How a person behaves, feels and thinks, how he conducts himself in a given set of circumstances is largely determined by the state of his mind. Mere external appearance or a person's speech or mannerisms are only fringes of one's personality. The real personality is reflected by the state of a person's mind, his thoughts, words, nature and actions.

The undisciplined mind acts as our enemy whereas a trained mind acts as our friend. The human mind has four basic functions: memory, deliberations and conceptualisation: detemination and decision making, and 'I' consciousness.

1. Memory: impressions of our thoughts/actions are stored.
2. Deliberation and conceptualisation: deliberation on many options and imagination, and formation of concepts.
3. Determination and decision making: discriminative faculty, responsible for decision making.
4. 'I' consicousness— appropriating to oneself all physical/mental activities.

The sum total of all our impressions (left by actions and thoughts) determines our character. The past has determined the present. Even so the present — our present thoughts and actions—will shape our future. This key principle governs personality development.

Strengthening of will power is the essence of personality development. Development involves struggle with your lower mind characterised by desires, old habits, wrong tendencies, impulses and bad impressions. The lesser we identify with the lower mind, the more we move towards the higher mind. This also makes us exercise our discrimination faculties, all culminating into a well developed personality with a refined character, high ideals, thoughts and goals.

Personality development must include

1. Faith in oneself.
2. Thinking positive thoughts.
3. Self-reliance.
4. Renunciation, service.
5. Correct attitude towards failures and mistakes.

A man aiming for success (either in worldly endeavours or spiritual field) must have a personality which has a well developed head, heart and hand! Not physically but in terms of:

1) head — great in mind; refined sensible positive thoughts.
2) heart — great in heart; service-oriented nature, a heart that feels intensely for the underprivileged, a heart that melts at the sorrows and miseries of the world.
3) hand — great hands, refering to great actions; a man who can perform great miracles, who can bring about a change for the good.

Thought, words, action and nature — all positive, service oriented, brimming with energy and vigour—make a personality perfect. These kinds of personalities achieve success. There are no failures, only setbacks is their attitude.

Have you seen the attitude of a weak, minded man? He does not confess his owns faults and weaknesses. He tries to hold himself faultless and lay the blame upon somebody or something else or even on bad luck. You should ask yourselves the question, why have I failed? This kind of self-enquiry and owning up can build your personality to a strong one. Great leaders, whose personalities stood out, had four important qualities in them:

1. Great thoughts
2. Stimulating words

3. Inspiring actions
4. Great nature.

So one izmportant factor for a well developed personality is (apart from good action, thoughts, words and nature) is taking or owning responsibility for a setback or failure if the fault lies in the self.

The ideal of all education and training lies in grooming a well developed personality. It entails building up good positive actions, inspiring words and thoughts and encouraging a positive nature; these are internal or interior polishing. There is no use in improving the external appearance (polishing one's outside) with 'aesthetic' instruments without an internal grooming. This will be like building a beautiful house without a foundation.

The important aspect in personality development that is often stressed is controlling 'fine' elements. This automatically brings removal of evils associated with 'gross elements'. A person must concentrate on aspects of subtle or fine elements in him. This immediately brings correction in his gross elements. There is a fearless, deathless, all moral, ethical, pure, divine bliss inside the core of each one of us. You must explore this. Instead of always being bodycentric you must try to understand and work on your finer elements. This is very important in personality development. You should aim for wisdom, and happiness in your life. Material success comes to that person who aims for higher things. Have you seen an athlete running on tracks to reach his 800 m mark? He crosses his 200m, 400m, 600m without any interest. Same is the case with the human beings aspiring for higher goals. Smaller success, fame, money, etc., come to them effortlessly but they are up to something great. Develop this attitude. Your personality shines like a bright solitaire if this is your attitude. You must go beyond pleasures and worldly achievements to enjoy real life.

Great scientists and leaders possessed strength of character and exteme levels of will power. One should imbibe such qualities from them.

'Give me a lever long enough and a place to stand and I will move the earth.'' (Archimedes I Ancient Greek Mathematician/physicist, 287-212 BC)

Character shaping or moulding includes accumulating good impressions in our mind. Each man's character is determined by the sum total of impressions in his mind. If good impressions prevail his character becomes good. If bad impressions are in excess, his character becomes bad. If a man continuously hears bad words, thinks bad thoughts, does bad actions, his mind will be full of bad impressions, They will influence his thought and work without his being conscious of the fact. In fact, these bad impresssions are always working, and their resultant effect must be evil, turning him into an evil man; he cannot help it. The sum total of these bad impressions will create the strong motive power for doing bad actions. Similarly, if a man has good thoughts and does good deeds, the impressions will be good and the sun total of these good impressions will force him to do good in spite of himself. 'Habit is second nature' goes the saying. The good impressions in the mind, coalesce and become a good habit. Habit thus becomes the first nature also and the whole nature of man—if good it becomes an asset and if bad it becomes a liability. Hence to shape our character we must see to it that impressions we are accumulating are good and for this we have to see, talk, think, hear, and do only good things. The result is good habits, good nature and ultimately good character. Character is repeated habits of good deeds that refine and reform you, important for all kinds of success.

Thoughts influence us. Fill yourselves with the good thoughts, creative, constructive ideas; whatever you do, think well on it. All your actions will be magnified, transformed, deified by the very power of the thought. Stay away from bad thoughts. Jealousy

- Non-violence
- Simplicity
- Patience
- Forbearance, selfcontrol

Mahatma Gandhi

- Courage
- Determination
- Service
- Conviction
- Intelligence and scientific temperament.

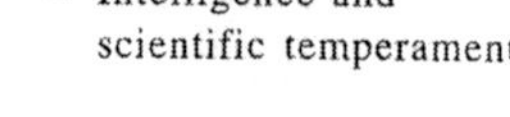

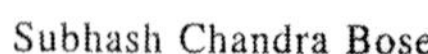

Subhash Chandra Bose

Learn the great qualities from the leaders we admire.

should never be entertained. Thoughts of envy can destroy you. Avoid grudging, resentful, envious thoughts. Entertain graceful, magnanimous, noble, generous thoughts. Your thoughts must be beneficent, benevolent, charitable, forgiving, human, kind, unselfish ideas. There must be thoughts of success, victory, fruitful profitable endeavours. Remember, life is short. Live it up to a great cause.

(B.Gita; Ch:II)
Verse 47

कर्मव्येगधिकारस्ते मा फलेषु कदाचन।
मा कर्मफलहेतुर्भू-र्मा ते सङ्गोऽस्त्वकर्मणि

In this verse Krishna's Motivating Message to mankind is:
To work alone you have the right, but never claim its result. Let not the results of actions be your motive nor be attached to action.

— 'Change, before changing.' The subjective world rules the objective. Change the subject and the object is bound to change. Purify yourself and the world is bound to be purified. A man who has control over himself cannot be affected upon by anything outside. The more we grow in love and virtue the more we see love and virtue outside. All condemnation of others really reflect on condemning ourselves. We cannot see outside what we are not inside. This very world will become to us an optimistic world when we become masters of our minds. Adjust the microcosm (yourself) and the macrocosm (world) will adjust itself for you.

****

16

Work and Selfless Actions

A 'responsible for' attitude makes you into a well developed personality. It instils leadership qualities. We are resposible for what we are. We have the power to make ourselves. Nothing makes us work so well at our best and highest as when all responsibility is thrown upon ourselves. You should be bold, strong and stand up to take the whole responsibility on your shoulders. This will make your realise that you are the creator of your own destiny. All the strength and succour you want is within yourself.

Responsible nature includes: ↓	*Outcome of a responsible action includes:* ↓
1. Being responsible for words, action.	Making you, your thoughts, worthwhile.
2. Accepting the blame as yours, if you are in the wrong.	Having your destiny in your hands.

3. Being accountable for the outcome of your performance
4. Being bold in taking a step.
5. Stepping forward in taking a challenge.

Work for work's sake. This should be the attitude. This

attitude makes you work without caring for money, name, fame. This work is aimed at bringing something good or beneficial to everyone. Unselfish work is more paying. Real activity according to the *Vedanta* is combined with eternal calmness and balance of mind. Work can be done in two ways. The second way is the way to SUCCESS

First way	*Second way*
Driven by passion .	**Calm; driven by selfless motives.**
Results:	**Results:**
1. Energy is wasted.	1. Energy is diverted to giving the best.
2. Nerve shattering stress.	2. Calm, composed, stress-free.
3. Disturbed mind.	3. Balanced minds.
4. Work unaccomplished.	4. Better work in quantity and quality.

The Karma Yoga of the *Gita* says that you should work with cleverness doing work as a science. All work is simply to bring out the power of the mind which is already there to wake up your soul. The power is inside every man. To the unattached (to results) all duties are equally good, and form efficient instruments with which selfishness and carnal pleasures may be destroyed, and the freedom of the soul secured. Every duty is holy, and devotion to duty is the highest form of the worship of God. Work is worship! Remember this golden saying.

You should work like a master and not as a slave. Work incessantly but do not do a slave's work. Work through freedom! Work through love! He works, who is not propelled by his own desires, by any selfishness whatsoever. He works who has no ulterior motive in view. He works who has no gain (selfish) from work!

Our duty to others mean's helping others, doing good to

the world. We should help the world and in the process help ourselves. When we help a man in distress, try to decrease his misery, the satisfaction, fulfilment and joy we derive gives a great motivation to us to do something better and higher, and upgrades our entire personality. So in helping others we are helping our own self. Selfless actions promote a healthy mind and a healthy body. We become forgetful of the ego when we think of the body as dedicated to the service of others, the body with which most complacently we identify the ego. The more intently you think of the well being of others, the more oblivious of the self you become. Ask nothing; want nothing in return when you help others. Give what you have to give; it will come back to you without expectation. Wisdom, knowledge, wealth, men, strength, prowess and whatever else nature gathers and provides us with are only for diffusion, when the moment of need is at hand.

All outgoing energy following a selfish motive is frittered away. It will not cause the power to return to you; but if restrained it will result in development of power. This self-control will tend to produce a mighty will, a character which makes a leader or a great man. Every successful man must have

tremendous integrity, tremendous sincerity and this is the cause of his signal success in life. He may not have been perfectly unselfish; yet he was tending towards it. If he had been perfectly unselfish his would have been as great a success as that of the Buddha or of Christ. The degree of unselfishness marks the degree of success everywhere.

****

17

Love, Faith and Learning

Love, sincerity, patience are the most essential qualities of success. Life is nothing but growth, expansion, love. All love is life and all selfishness is death. This is the law of nature.

It is life to do good to others, it is death not to do good to others. You should feel for the poor, the ignor the downtrodden. This heart felt sympathy and the love emanating subsequentlywill render power, help and indomitable energy. Those who have no feelings in the heart for the impoverished are like a wild beast! If in this hell of a world one can bring a little joy and peace even for a day into the heart of a single person, that much alone is true. All else is mere deception.

Crush the fear!

The weak have no place in this world. Weakness leads to

slavery and all kinds of misery, physical and mental. Weakness is death. Strength is life. Weakness is constant strain and misery. Strength is felicity and bliss. With weakness comes ignorance and with ignorance comes misery. Let positive, strong, helpful thoughts pervade your mind always as this gives extreme strength—the will power and energy to fight all the battles of life. You must avoid 'weakness' like the plague and unleash the infinite strength and power coiled up inside your mind and body. Fear and weakness go hand in hand. Avoid fear; crush it and it vanishes. Be not afraid; one must go on bravely. Bravery and strength are the ultimate weapons for success.

Let the world say what it chooses, I shall tread the path of duty. Know this to be the line of action for you to take. Those who are always downhearted and dispirited in this life can do no work. To be a 'hero' you should be fearless, righteous and positive. A true hero is unaffected by happiness or misery, prosperity and adversity. He knows them all to be of momentary duration. He ignores them and walks ahead in pursuit of his goal. Be a hero, not a zero!

Your faith in yourself is the most perfect motive power which can almost make you achieve anything. Great leaders, heroes, scientists became great only by the faith they had in their potentials and talents. If a man hates himself degeneration will be his fate. Nothing can change it! He who has no faith in himself can never achieve anything. Whatever you think, that you will be. Think yourselves as strong, successful and assertive, and you will become one. Believe in yourself, your potential, capacity, and miracles can happen. The history of the world is the history of a few men who had faith in themselves. That faith calls out for the divinity within. You can do anything. You fail only when you do not strive sufficiently to manifest infinite power. As soon as a man or a nation loses faith, death comes.

Learn! There is no end to learning and updating your knowledge. The man who says he has nothing more to learn is al-

Sudha Murthy
Chairperson of Infosys Writer, social worker

- Many of the computer software professionals and engineers look up to her as their ideal.
- She is worth emulating.
- One should aim at following ideals such as hers.

ready at his last grasp. The nation that says it knows everything is on the very brink of destruction! Your motto should be: 'As long as I live so long will I learn'. Learn and update your knowledge, staying abreast with the rest of the world. A doctor should know what is happening in his field, otherwise he will be out of practice. Unless he goes through medical journals, attends seminars, listens to lectures in CME (continuing medical education) programmes he will not be aware of the latest developments in medical specialities and will become outdated in knowledge and techniques. When we learn anything from others we must mould it to suit our own purpose. 'No imitations, no copying.' This is a important rule to remember. Successful men don't, do different, things, they do things differently, is the dictum. Anything you do must have your originality. Imitation never makes for progress. Learn everything that is good from others, but bring it in and in your own way absorb it; do not become others. Learn the right things and be yourself, incorporating the good of what you have learnt into your actions, thoughts, words.

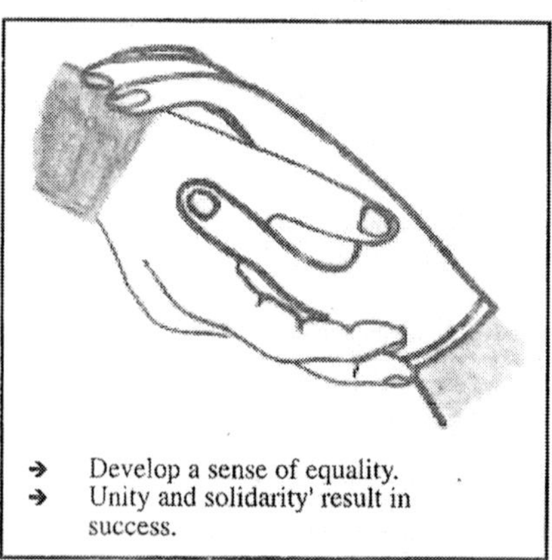

➔ Develop a sense of equality.
➔ Unity and solidarity' result in success.

We all learn so many

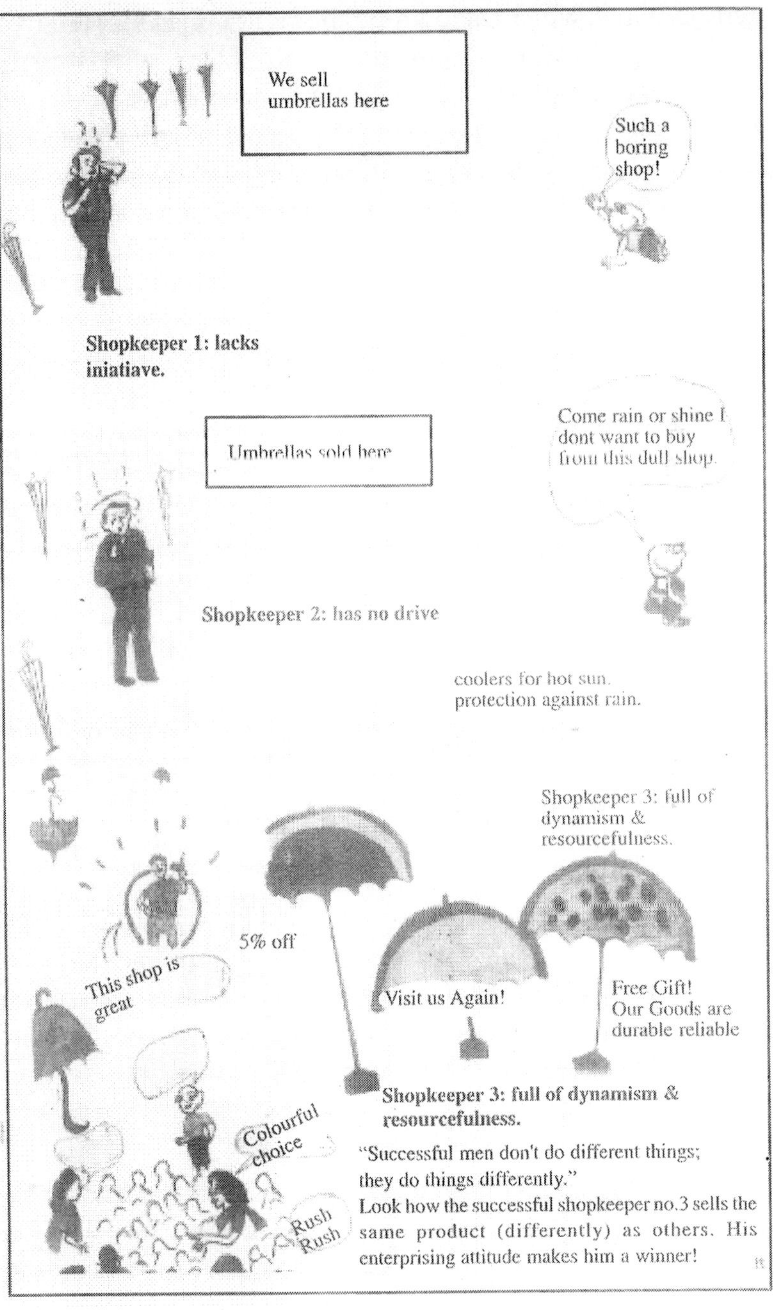

"Successful men don't do different things; they do things differently."

Look how the successful shopkeeper no.3 sells the same product (differently) as others. His enterprising attitude makes him a winner!

wrong things when it should be the right things that are to be learnt. From Western countries we learn their way of dressing, smoking, drinking and dancing to pop music. We should learn their neatness, "earn while you learn" kind of self-sufficiency, dignity of labour and 'live and let live' attitude. We want to ape the foreigners in their lifestyle and in that frenzy we are prepared to sacrifice our country, parents, customs, traditions and values. 'Brain drain' resulting from the new 'Quit India' slogan of today for students has become a routine now. Every year thousands of doctors and engineers, after utilising their country resources in completing their education, rush to Western countries for money, comforts and free lifestyles. One needs to learn the good points from Western countries and must contribute to one's own great country by being productive and patriotic. India needs youngsters, motivated and high spirited and at the same time who can preserve India's great culture, traditions and values. Nobody is against variation. Variation is the sign of life. Sameness is the sign of stagnation and death. Each must assimilate the spirit of others, learn the positive attributes from others, yet preserve his individuality and grow according to his own law of growth. He must also realise his responsibility towards his family, society and country.

Certain ethics are to be practised for a righteous life. Strength, independence, love, faith, knowledge, selfless nature are all basic ethics. Weakness, dependence, hate, doubt, ignorance selfish motives are all unethical. One of the most important ethics to be followed, whether in working place or in other places, is to recognise the oneness in all the beings. Diversity and discrimination are sins. Practise what you preach; first have faith in self, be helpful and loving — all these ethics followed will eventually pay way for success.

The one great first step for any success is to hold on to the ideal. A person must have a clearcut idea about his ideal. He must think, dream, live on that ideal. Struggles and turmoils on the way to achieving the ideal must not divert you from your pursuit. The life of the practical is in the ideal. It is the ideal that has made us what we are, and will make us what we are going to be.

All success in any line of work is the result of one's power of concentration. High achievement in art, music, etc., is the result of concentration. Man alone has the greater power of concentration among all living beings. We must learn not only to attach the mind to one thing exclusively but also detach it at a moment's notice and place it on something else. These two should be developed together to make it safe. Otherwise we will end up being obsessed with the concentrated thing and end up in suffering. Systematic, methodical development of the mind is the need. Concentrate and focus on positive things and attributes. The power of concentration is infinite. The human mind can achieve wonders with the power of concentration (on right things, of course).

Develop the sense of equality. A strong brain, clear mind free of nonsensical ideas and superstitions, realises that all perfections and powers are within one's own 'self' and these have not been given to him by others. Having realised 'this' one becomes free and achieves equality. A person also realises that everyone else is equally as perfect as he, and he does not have to exercise any power physical, mental or moral — over his brethren. He has to abandon the idea that there is any man lower than himself. Then he can talk of equality, not until then.

Learn to feel yourself in other bodies, to know that we are all one. Do not repent, or brood over past deeds or dwell on your good deeds. This is the only way to attain an unattached free state of mind. Feeling of non-attachment gives you 'freedom' — freedom from selfish and selfless preoccupations. A free mind neither cries over misery and defeat nor rejoices over happiness and success. A liberated' mind breaks the shackles of difference and basks in the light of sameness, revelling in the joy of equality. He who has succeeded in detaching his mind from the centres at will has succeeded in "gathering towards" checking the outgoing powers of the mind, framing it from the thraldom of the senses. Having done this he achieves "strength of character" and "indomitable personality".

Even the least thing well done brings marvellous results. Therefore, let everyone do what little he can. You must go beyond the concepts of body, mind, intellect and realise the atman, the spirit lodged inside everyone — all pervading and indissoluble. Such a realisation provides infinite fearlessness. This propels us, drives us, motivates us to march on, to succeed! The message is loud and clear 'Arise, awake, and stop not till the goal is reached!'

****

18

Success Mantras

Success will not come or fall in our lap spontaneously. One has to plan. Work and plan intelligently to get success in your endeavours. Hindu mythology speaks of 'Bhagiratha' who worked really hard to bring the river Ganges to the earth, and of Dhruva who had to sweat, toil and do extraordinary things to attain the status of a celestial star. Nothing comes easy. Mythology talks about their clearcut goals, penance in harsh conditions and determination before they achieved their targets.

Whether it is the microsoft Bill Gates or our Indian top business tycoons—Tatas, Ambanis or Narayana Murthy–all have worked hard to achieve their success. They are a source of motivation to thousands of aspiring youngsters. Basically all have followed the 10 golden steps to success.

1. *Basic aim, goal or destination:* This must be the first step. You should have a target. Unless you have an ambition, aim or goal you cannot work. Farhan Akhtars film 'Lakshya' talks about this very beautifully. If you have decided clearly on your ambition or aim nothing is impossible. You cannot light a lamp without oil. Similarly you cannot succeed without an aim.

2. *Try to have an individuality and originality in your field.* Have

complete knowledge of your chosen field. You must be able to solve all the doubts arising in the minds of juniors or subordinates and colleagues pertaining to your field of excellence. Winds and waves become conducive to only that sailor who is an expert in navigation. Similarly, your staff can help you only if you are competent.

3. *Self-confidence and faith in self is very important.* Only with high levels of self-confidence can you succeed. Have you seen the successful people? Take, for example, the Ambanis. They are oozing with self-confidence. They can take charge of any situation by the faith they have in themselves. Self-confidence, self-assurance alone can help you succeed. The great teacher Dronacharya was amazed by the self-confidence of Ekalavya who excelled in archery.
4. *Attitude is important.* Have a winner's attitude. You should always have a winning approach. and a winning spirit in you. Thoughts, words, action all must be aimed at victory.
5. *Be bold.* You should be daring, striking, strong and vivid in all the steps taken. Any venture must be taken up with brave, adventurous bent of mind. Brave, bold steps taken yield success in right measures.
6. *Make decisions.* You should decide clearly and with determination, never postpone decisions. Never procrastinate. Delays in decision making can destroy many a chance to succeed. Decision should be on the basis of now or never! This does not mean a hasty decision. You can think, weigh the pros and cons, judge and make a decision if you have the will do it. There is a lot of difference between making a hasty decision and making a quick dicision. Hasty decision is impulsive, careless and can precipitate failures. Quick decision is speedy, swift, brisk and conclusive. Quick decisions avert many problems and accidents and assure success.

7. *Learn to respect the work of others.* Understand the dignity of labour. Time is precious both for you and your employees, the employees or unions. If the expectation wavelength of an employee and action plan wavelength of boss, match, success is sure to come.

8. *Never waste an opportunity.* Advantageous, favourable chances should never be wasted. Suitable, timely, appropriate opportunities knocking at your doorstep must be welcomed with outstretched hands. Make use of it.

9. *The customer is always right.* You can win an argument but you will lose your client if you try to outsmart him. Listen and comprehend what others have to say. Make yourself clear and comprehensible. Whatever you say must be well defined, unambiguous, definite and unmistakable.

10. *Success to begin with is elusive.* It eludes, escapes, gets away from and gives a person the slip in the initial stages of struggle. There is lot of pain, strain, stress when the efforts fail. The secret is 'Never give up'! You should cultivate the strength to survive the initial disappointments, battle, competition, comparisons, exertion, fight and toil. Slowly the success begins to materialise. It comes into your stronghold. There is a volte face—struggle becomes an effortless, relaxing endeavour. There is gain, joy, profits, genial, pleasant experiences and peace everywhere. Efforts begin to pay heftily. You begin to realise your dreams; a battle becomes a party; competitions and comparisons become healthy challenges; exertion, fight and toil turn into pleasure, harmony and leisure.

What is the similarity between gold, sugarcane and bamboo? All have to undergo severe, rigorous changes before ending up as unadulterated, uncontaminated, absolutely pure ornaments; crystals and cubes of sugar; melodious flute. To get a fine outcome the initial process has to be severe and harsh. The same thing applies to life. You have to undergo a lot of toil, sweat and struggle; only then can you smell the sweet scent of success!

****

Part-IV

MANAGEMENT

19

Success Strategies

To achieve a blueprint for success, you must go through various materials—books, articles, autobiographies, films and personal study. Containing motivating aspects from the lives of various popular personalities they are sure to contain some clue, some method which can be accepted as a time tested, proven success method. You must learn and use these clues or methods to achieve success in your endeavours. You must have the real will to succeed, and if you really care about your success you will definitely be serious about it. This seriousness will make you use the proven success methods persistently and consistently. A person may want different things in life. It can be a life goal, it can be a problem (his or of others) which he may want to solve; it can be mental peace; it can be a wish to become like a famous person (someone he worships, adores, admires and follows). By learning the motivating aspects from the lives of successful men and success strategies you can definitely attain what you wants to in life or from life.

If we go through the success stories of men and women who are now in top positions, we often find certain common features. One such feature is the 'Try Harder' concept. You have to try harder—better than your present efforts—to achieve your goal. You are bound to attain the goal (you desire) in life much faster if your present situation or the magnitude of your goal forces you or motivates you to try harder! Certain difficulties serve as catalysts and makes you try hard. People with difficulties often have no motivation and find themselves strck in complacency. Difficulties and challenges serve as 'try extra hard' catalysts and result in the development of terrific success momentum. So get that extra drive to reach out to your life goal. 'Try harder' or that one 'extra last push' is a success clue seen in biographies of many successful men.

People have a self- image and become what they envision themselves to be. Envision means to mentally picture. You must constantly mentally picture yourself as being what you want to become. To be successful, famous, rich, you must mentally picture yourself as being successful, famous rich. You cannot succeed if you mentally pictures yourself as a failure. 'Think Big' and achieve that magnitude, say celebrities and popular figures. It is a proven concept that your thoughts—which you inwardly see as mental pictures—control your life and determine your future. These thoughts form the mental blueprint that directs how your life will be built. Your mental picture becomes a reality when the subconscious mind receives enough persistent instructions and finally guides your life in the direction of your mental picture. The *Bible,* says' 'As a man thinketh, so is he'. The subconscious mind converts the mental pictures into reality by its intense power. The lives of famous personalities stress time and again the importance of thoughts. You must thus remember that 'your future will be what you mentally picture it be'. You become what you most frequently think (and mentally picture) you will be. You must guide your life with mental pictures. Just as the mental pictures are nothing but your thoughts, mental movies are continuous sequence of your thoughts. If these are projected on the screen of your subconscious mind, the intense power of this mind converts these into reality. If you think you are successful, play your thoughts of success again and again in your subconscious mind.

Over a period of time the mind guides you in the direction of success and it becomes a reality — a real success! Most of the success stories talk about (1) the conscious mind which makes decisions consciously regarding your aims, ambitions and desires (2) the subconscious mind which accepts the mental pictures formed by the conscious mind and have its power guide you in moving towards your goal or aim (3) the infinite mind which is the total intelligence of the universe, all pervading. This infinite mind, called, Soul or God, can be communicated with prayers.

****

20
Motivational Guidance

In success training programmes motivational guidance means the subconscious mind's power to direct your life towards your aims or goals (which were projected as mental pictures) so that they turn into reality. Imagination can also be used to produce powerful mental pictures. You must respond to such guidance from the subconscious mind. At the same time your must turn off the unwanted negative mental pictures (worries, anxieties, fears, guilt complexes). This can be done by mental relaxation techniques which entirely obscure all uncontrolled mental pictures. A quiet

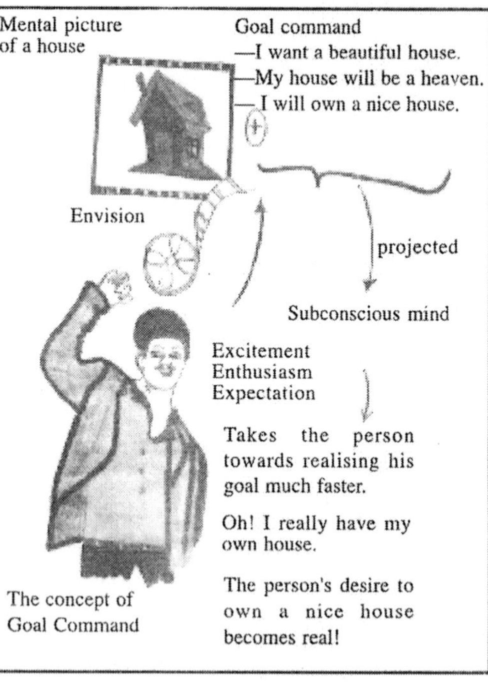

The concept of Goal Command

mind can be achieved by relaxing slowly the body-face-eyes, blanking out all mental pictures. Yoga, meditation and various ancient techniques can help you in achieving such relaxation and tranquillity.

Next comes intensifying the mental pictures. You can intensify the mental pictures of your goal or whatever you want by various psychological methods. Goal command is an important method to intensify the mental pictures. In goal command you mentally repeat, what you want again and again. For example, if you have aimed at being rich, your mental picture will be of wealth, money, comforts, etc. To intensify this mental picture you have to use words (mentally). To emphasise what you want (here wealth or riches) you can use the command. 'Make a crore'!

You have to repeat this command mentally over and over at every opportunity. Make a crore! Make a crore! These commands repeated mentally hundred or thousand times a day, at every available instance will emphasize the mental picture and command the subconscious mind to guide you towards your desire or goal. Goal commands can be used to command your subconscious mind to produce whatever you want.

Mental Picture

Happiness

Love

Power

Fame

Goal Command

Make me happy.

I want love.

I want power.

Make me famous.

Another way to intensify your mental pictures is by excitement. You can activate your mental pictures by being excited about your life goal. Excitement stirs emotions. Excitement motivates enthusiasm.

Added		**Goal Command**
Excitement	—mental picture	—Quicker guidance
Enthusiasm	of goal	from the
Expectation		subconscious mind towards the goal. Quicker translation of mental picture to reality.

You should constantly repeat your goal command to your subconscious in exciting intense mental pictures emphasized by a simultaneous forceful word command. Constant repetition can make the goal command dominant in your daily thought. This is called goal command reemphasis. Just as you cannot take a picture with your camera unless you expose the film to whatever you want in your picture you cannot make a mental picture unless you expose your mind to whatever you want to mentally picture. Our thoughts are mental pictures. Thoughts are very patent. Buddha said "All that we are is the result of what we have thought." Marcus Aurelius said, "Our life is what thoughts make it." Therefore, your mental pictures are of great of importance to you because they will become your life! You should expose your mind to whatever you want in life. The mind camera will make a mental picture of whatever is exposed to it.

You must constantly expose your mind to the desired objects to get the desired mental pictures. These are to be projected on the subconsious mind. You should expose your mind to success opportunities. If you flood your subconscious with constituent, constant, intense mental pictures of success you will activate the vast power of your subconscious to materialise those consistent, constant intense mental pictures. When you fill the subconscious with mental pictures of success, your subconscious fills your life with success!

Psychologists explain these methods of success very methodically, step by step. But in real life, in the lives of many successful men these methods have happened very spontaneously without any planning. To put it in simple words, most of the successful men have envisioned themselves to be a success, and without much conscious efforts have again and again drilled these thoughts into their minds. Success materialised to them one fine day!

A person either makes a very conscious, step by step, methodical planned effort to achieve what he wants to, or he can just go about doing his efforts with a single spontaneous (unplanned) thought of success; in both these cases success materialises.

Now you should make a constant companion of your ideal self-image. First you must decide what you would like to be in the future. Make that your ideal self-image. Then imagine that your ideal self-image is your constant companion, your invisible friend, your helpful advisor. You must make it mentally real. You must always live up to the ideals of your finest self-image. You can also have conversations (mentally) with your ideal self.

Psychologists suggest so many methods and techniques for such concepts. Self-hypnosis and many techniques help in such attempts. But to put it in simple words there are three basic steps.

1) Imagine your ideal self.
2) Make him your companion. Live up to his standards
3) When you start living up to the standards of your ideal self, temptations and faults associated with you vanish; the ideal merges with you. Your ideal becomes real! When

you merge with your ideal self-image, you become ideal yourself.

Remember people becomewhat they mentally picture themselves to be.

Buddha's quiet mind must be our inspiration.

Quiet mind is acheived by eye relaxation. Blank out or black out all eye emotions.

Most top personalities point out that you must master your problems or the problems will end up mastering you. 'Attack is the best form of defence' strategy. You must keep a quiet mind._This helps to solve all the problems calmly, intelligently and logically. A quiet mind maintains mental command over problems. A quiet mind in a crisis is like the eye of a hurricane. In a hurricane, destructive winds whirl violently except in the centre (the 'eye') of the hurricane which is a place of absolute calm in the very centre of the destructive forces all around it.

Psychologists and many yoga therapists, and relaxation technique therapists say there is a very close relationship between one's eyes and mind. This action-reaction between the eyes and the mind includes physical and emotional aspects. The eyes respond to the mind-moods (emotions). They weep in grief, flash with anger, etc., They not only respond to emotions but also escalate the emotions to which they respond and express. By relaxing the intensity of your eye emotions you can calm the emotions and achieve a quiet mind. This eye control is achieved by becoming 'consciously aware' and then the eyes focus on the emotion so that relaxation by restraint of mind control is achieved through eye relaxation first. Eye relaxation or blanking out all eye emotions will slowly bring about relaxation of mind. A quiet mind is achieved at last.

You should examine your problems and troubles with a calm, reasoning judgement of a quiet mind. You must never emotionalise your troubles. You must be impassively serene, resigned to be inevitably submissively patient. Accept it! Emotional outbursts in response to any kind of trouble or problems lower the resistance to the next problem and get shattered (break down). Troubles or problems should not be escalated by emotion. Instead, troubles should be handled with a gentle touch. Problems should be tackled with a calm approach. Suppose you are given a beautiful flower vase with a 'crack'. Do you repair it with a hammer? No! we repair it with an adhesive gently. Similarly, problems need not be dealt with emotional hammers; they need to be corrected with calm and composure adhesives!

To keep a quiet mind one must not over-react. The great French philosopher, Montaigne, said, "A man is not hurt so much by what happens to him—as by his opinion of what happens." It is not what happens but how one feels about it, which really matters to him. Over-reaction is principally caused by over-sensitive feelings. To prevent over-reacting you should stop being over-sensitive. The way to stop being over-sensitive begins with acceptance of the fact that people, things, situations and events are not perfect. Nor are they provided for one's personal approval or pleasure. You cannot demand perfection or personally attempt to make perfect an obviously imperfect world, filled with obviously imperfect people and imperfect situations. You must accept the imperfections of others as you hope they will accept your own imperfections. You should stop being over-sensitive to imperfection and not overreact. The rule is to develop the serene attitude of acceptance to what cannot be changed!

All negative emotions can exhaust a person completely. Anger is a mark of weakness. It means "being hurt.... and wincing" are the famous words of the philosopher, Marcus Aurelius. You must get tough emotionally and stop being a weak, emotionally thin skinned, easily hurt, individual. You must adopt the following two strategies to deal with incidental offences and side remarks.

1. Ignoring it! General Eisenhower said he never wasted a minute thinking about people he didn't like.
2. Turn it off, using the 'relaxing the eyes' or blanking out all emotion techniques. Turn off your emotions.

Next comes dealing with resentment. Resentment is trouble in past tense. Whatever caused one resentment already has happened and therefore cannot be undone. Since the past cannot be changed and the event cannot be altered you must adopt the following methods to alleviate the torture of resentment.

1. Change your attitude toward the cause of your resentment.
2. Forget it! Confucius said, "To be wronged is nothing — unless you continue to remember it."

No situation can be improved by your resentment. It can only be made worse. Resentment leads to a chain reaction of anger, hate, hostility evidence. So you must get rid of resentment before it leads to something worse.

****

21
Anger Management Tips

It is very easy to control but very difficult to transform anger. You can contol your anger but in that process you suppress it. When suppressed the direction of movement changes. It was going out and when suppressed it starts going in. Healthy anger release must be done in the following ways:

1. You must recognise the anger you are feeling. Anger may be denied because you feel too guilty about it or afraid of it and as a result the feeling is turned inwards or inside where it festers.

2. You must decide what made you angry. You must think whether this is worth getting angry over. If it is a small annoyance that pressed the angry button, forget it, is the

rule. If you cannot forget it then the source of your anger goes beyond this simple incident. You must ferret out the underlying cause of your hostility. You must bring your feeling to the surface and deal with it.

3. Your should give the provoker the benefit of the doubt. Instead of inflaming your anger by feeding yourself with negative thoughts you must suggest to yourself that this person is having a bad day. You must come up with a reasonable justification for the behaviour of the provoker, something that you can understand and relate to.
4. Counting ten or practising some form of mental relaxation. You must first calm down, then discuss the conflict rationally.
5. You should make your grievance known without attacking the other person. This calls for tact and some good communication skills. One important tip. You must register your complaint using yourself instead of the other person.
6. You must listen hard and, above all, understand. This is the key to resolve a conflict,

and resolving the conflict is after all the key to safety, diffusing your anger.

7. Forgive. When a person forgives someone (and this may include his very own self) many clearly positive psychological and physiological changes take place. He feels warm, his blood pressure and heart rate drop, and he may even cry. But most importantly, through forgiveness he once again experiences the love that is the essence of retationship.
8. Yoga therapists prescribe shashankasana, paschimottanasana, koormasana; pranayama techniques like nadi shodhana and bhramari as a remedy for anger.

You must stop resentment at its source, by considering its source... with sympathetic understanding. Always understand that every slight annoyance is not intentional, and completely ignore it. You can shrug it off as being too insignificant or just laugh at it. Then you should forget it. Sooner or later you are going to forget the minor annoyances which today cause you irritation and resentment. Why not do it as early as possible so that a lot of useful energy can be conserved and channelised to constructive purposes?

Anger is self-destructive and should be avoided at any cost. Pythagoras said, "Anger begins in folly and ends in repentance." You must remember the proverb, "He who can suppress a moment's anger may prevent a day of sorrow." Anger only escalates an existing problem. A person who loses his temper at every situation slowly turns into an 'anger addict' and this drains him physically, mentally and emotionally. Anger addiction is as dangerous as drug or alcohol addiction. The rule to remember as far as anger is concerned is "Prevention is better than cure." If the anger disease has already come the remedy is delay it! When angry, count to ten before you speak and if very angry, count to a hundred. This is the time-tested successful remedy for the treatment of anger. By keeping cool, one keeps control, control over both him and others. This in turn controls the entire circumstances. Forgive is the treatment which can be used when you want to avoid or treat anger. Forgiveness the person who angers you, whose actions or words anger you. This keeps you calm and you retain peace of mind. Always value a quiet mind as it can help you in avoiding anger and save your energy.

****

22
Optimism

Worry is self-torture and you must not subject yourself to it. There is no point in worrying over adversities. Some of them will never even happen to you. Some which may happen will not be as disastrous (as worried) and some cannot be prevented by worrying! Worrying never prevents anything from happening! You cannot worry your troubles away! So you must stop worrying!

In dealing with negative emotions you should never escalate a negative emotion. Always put a 'full stop' to all the negative emotions. Whether it is resentment, anger, dislike, hatred, worry—you must never escalate or heighten it. Put a firm stop to all these emotions. Never entertain them. Develop the attitude of stopping them at their very inception. They will disappear. Always believe in the saying,

"When fate closes one door, faith always opens another." This is a highly dependable dictum.

Never hurry! Hurry in doing anything and everything leads to frustration and worry. The really big achievers value time but do not hurry. They do their tasks unhurriedly, one at a time, and complete each task one at a time, unhurriedly!

Many a biography or autobiography of great people lists four basic essences of their experiences and life (1) Always speak softly, pleasantly but firmly (2) Never speak harsh, irritating, caustic words (3) Do not overreact in anger (4) Do not act rashly. A wise man can easily follow these four principles and can make a big change (for good) in his life.

Many famous personalities attribute their fame and success to being mentally well balanced when emotionally disturbing situations happened. You must never over-react to emotionally disturbing situations. Some people react and over-react to something which has not even happened! Imagining disasters, tragedies, troubles—some people over react! Isn't it ridiculous to imagine horrible things and over-react to it unnecessarily. Never entertain such imagined troubles may upset that you. Never get emotionally disturbed or over-react imagining a disastrous future with burdens of trouble and tragedies. Live in the present! Take each day as it comes.

— One has to have this 'Hope for the best, be prepared for the worst' attitude.
— In the above case this man has to present his project— It may get approved; appreciated & admired.

(or)

It may be rejected; abused and berated.
He has prepared himself for both the eventualities. He will receive both the bouquet & brickbat with the same poise.

Be optimistic and enthusiastic. Each day is a gift from God! Enjoy it!

One important point which everybody must learn is to be prepared for any troubles that may come. You should not over-react or worry over imagined disasters. At the same time you must prepare yourself mentally, emotionally and spiritually to cope with whatever troubles may come. Remember the golden words: Hope for the best, be prepared for the worst!

You must prudently prepare so that you are not overwhelmed by events which may rush upon you like a flood of troubled waters. Just as a dam constructed well in advance prevents a devastating flood, preparing yourself against any unforeseen consequence will help in giving resistance, strength and skill to deal with it if (at all) and when it strikes all of a sudden. You must raise the height of your nervous or emotional threshold so that you can deal with any catastrophe or disaster (which may unnerve you or drain you emotionally) coming all of a sudden. You must be always 'ready' in your mind for emergencies and contingencies 'Faith can serve as an effective rescue boat in any troubled waters. Faith in self and God! If you have it you can tackle any situation.

Be less criticising and more sympathising. Criticising turns people off! Sympathising turns people on!

Sympathising combines understanding, agreement and emotional acceptance. Sympathy helps you to become popular and wins you love and friendship. Criticism cultivates hurt, hatred, hostility. To influence people you must do less criticising and noresympathising. To succeed do less criticising and more sympathising. When people realise that you are sympathetic to their—goals, cause, beliefs, hopes and ideals they gladly help you to attain a higher position because by doing so they are putting you in a better position to help them attain their goals, seek their cause, work for their belief, hopes and ideals.

When sympathy is used in its total meaning of understanding, agreement and emotional acceptance, it becomes a vital ingredient to express love and saves sacred institutions like marriage. Many divorces are the result of the belief that he/she doesn't sympathize with my problems, feelings, etc., and therefore he does not really love me. Genuine sympathy safeguards the sacrosanct institution of marriage.

Never underestimate the power of genuinely expressed sympathy. Never overestimate the power of criticism. It can be harmful and ruin many a friendship, marriage and success.

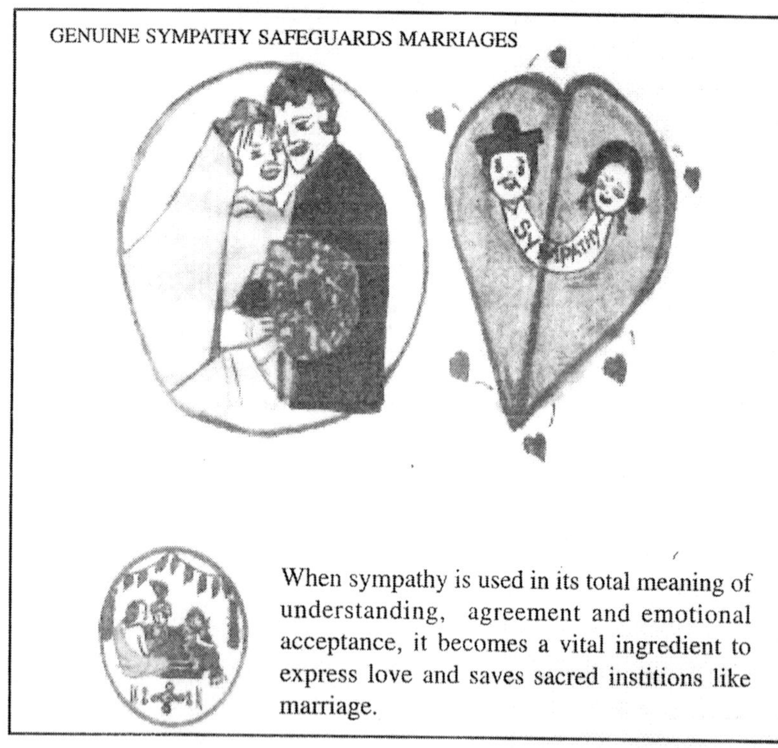

GENUINE SYMPATHY SAFEGUARDS MARRIAGES

When sympathy is used in its total meaning of understanding, agreement and emotional acceptance, it becomes a vital ingredient to express love and saves sacred institions like marriage.

Do it your-self people are seen all around. Many are self - proclaimed authorities and experts on subjects concerning which they have only limited knowledge. There is nothing wrong in being self-sufficient or reliant. The man who says I do everything

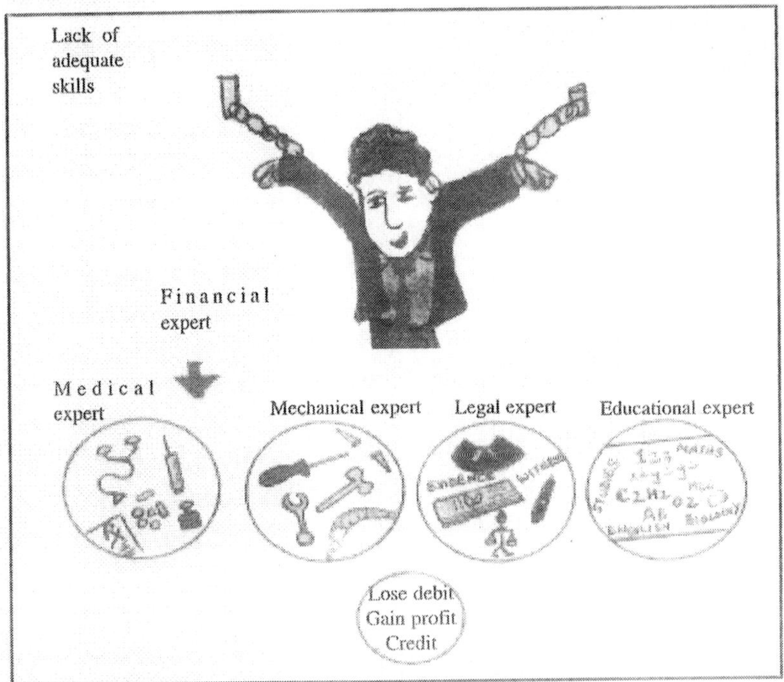

by myself, I believe in doing everything with my own hands' is commendable no doubt. But he must know his limitations. When a task requires specialised knowledge, technical training, exceptional skill, professional abilities—which he does not have— he must let the experts do it. Delegation is the secret. What he can do well he should do. What needs an expert's job should not be attempted and should be left to the expert. The services of highly qualified experts in specialised endeavours are always worth more than they cost. When he knows that he is incapable of doing a particular job he should opt for an expert immediately. His savings in time, money, trouble and worry will be enormous. He should realise that no sizable fortune ever has been amassed without the help of experts. You must realise that experts are available for every specialised task but there is only one master— God. You need. His blessings and support in all tasks—small or big. Reach out to Him with prayers and sincerity and His support is assured.

Developing the power of patience is an important point to be remembered. You have to be patient to achieve whatever you want. Joseph De Maistre, the great French writer, said, "To know how to wait is the great secret of success." When you exercise your sublimest power of simple patience, you achieve great things. Most of the successful people recommend that a steady, patient, persevering thinking will generally surmount every obstacle in the path of success. Napoleon said, "Victory belongs to the persevering." Patience, perseverence and persistence are the three P' one must firmly adhere to. Once you acquire these three qualities success comes to you very easily. All the things in this world are obtainable if you wait patiently.

"Whatever man can conceive and believe, he can acheive" is the law of life. You must realise your power. You should make

Ingredients for success recipe

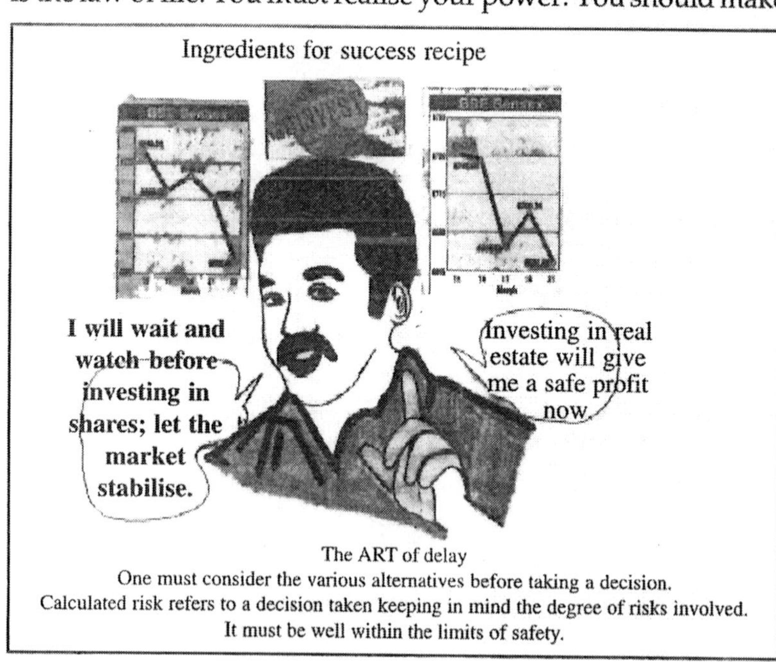

The ART of delay

One must consider the various alternatives before taking a decision. Calculated risk refers to a decision taken keeping in mind the degree of risks involved. It must be well within the limits of safety.

attempts with the available power to achieve what you want. You should never depend on something or somebody to come and help you in your attempts. When you start ttempting and doing things on your own with a firm belief in God and faith in your power and capabilities, you become an instant success! Each and every person must develop this power to attempt and do things with faith and this takes him towards his goal briskly. Never hesitate, start doing, start attempting and see the power within you increasing mani fold. This is the advice of most successful personalities.

It is important to realise that your positive nature alone cannot bring you great success or even a mediocre success, without the goodwill and cooperation of other people. People will not lift you to success unless you have made a favourable impression on them and successfully influenced them to want to help you. You too should influence and motivate others to success. You need to make attempts and efforts on your own but also have the goodwill and cooperation of people around you. No man is an island. You need everybody in your attempts and ventures to succeed.

****

23

Tolerance and Moderation

People, places, situations, events, emotional feelings are all relative. They are good or bad in degree—depending upon with what they are compared with. This kind of comparison and then arriving at a judgement will teach you tolerance and moderation. You become more level- headed. You don't make triumphs out of modest accomplishments or disasters out of minor disappointments. You develop equipoise. When we compare our beautiful, expensive house to a charitable home or hospital we realise our selfishness. Certain situations or events which seem a disaster at the first look, become not all that bad when compared to a past or possible event which was or can be a catastrophe. All these comparisons teach us moderation. Many happenings judged with over-reactions and emotions make you a hyper. But when these happenings are compared to similar happenings in the past or present and judged unemotionaly without over-reaction they become a trivia. Thus comparison, weighing and judging are tools for achieving tolerance and moderation.

Most of the successful men prescribe two important ingredients for success recipe:

1. Say 'No' generally.
2. Say 'Yes' selectively.

You most say 'No' generally to everything which would be a significant distraction from your concentrated thought and effort to reach your main goal. And you must say 'Yes' very selectively only to the offers and requests which are compatible with your main goal. By saying 'no' to many things desirable but irrelevant, you clear the 'yes' road directly to your goal in life.

The art of delaying also ensures success to a certain degree. You must never rush rashly in your attempts and efforts. Whatever is done should be done with thoughtful, disciplined and intended skill. When something has to be done one must consider all the available alternatives. This docs not mean you should entertain laziness. You must restrain your over-eagerness, impulsive-instant-rash acting urge and should stick to more judgement. Here comes the question of what is risk and what is calculated risk. What is delay and what is pure laziness? One must never rush into ventures without weighing the pros and cons. This is risk. On the other hand, if you carefully weigh the pros and cons, calculate, plans and then venture— it is calculated risk. Delay refers to anything done with caution, not mere prolonging. Laziness is pure unwillingness to attempt or work. One should practise the art of delay—calmly considering all alternative choices before venturing. It is better to Do It Right than to Do It Now.

Most success stories prescribe a combination of Desire + Belief+ Expectancy to achieve one's life goal and success. You must intensely desire your life goal and deeply believe that you will attain your life goal. You must confidently expect that he will surely achieve it. Three attributes are ways to your goal or success. Referred to as the three G's, these three qualities make you popular, successful and happy with the people around you.

1) You must always express your gratitude.
2) You must always express your goodwill.

3) You must always express you good wishes .

When a person expresses his gratitude, goodwill and good wishes to every person (without exception), he will radiate happiness and friendship to all others, without deliberately seeking any selfish gain from each, but just the happiness it will give them. When this is done, it leaves an impressive, memorable image of him in the minds of people and they reciprocate. As you sow, so shall you reap goes the saying. When you unselfishly practise these virtues, you become popular, you are appreciated by one and all, and in time you become a success figure.

It is more blessed to give than to receive teaches the *Bible.* The true art of giving is in not expecting and not wanting anything in return. But there is an even greater act. It is the art of giving and graciously accepting something in return. When you receive something in return graciously without selfish benefits you give a lot of satisfaction to the person who gives you the return gifts. Have you seen the happiness in the face of a small birthday child giving return gifts? This is worth a world. Nothing should be taken or given with selfish motives. Done graciously both these give and, take acts become a bliss. Successful people have practised this technique and have won their battles with this art of gracious giving and gracious receiving. Thanksgiving done to God must be with utmost sincerity and gratitude. Its power is infinite!

The biographies of successful figures, stress the importance of unstoppable movement forward. You should never stop or back. You should never look back out. You must fix your life's goal and having done it must charter out a channel leading to it. You must keep moving forward in that channel. 'Keep the ball rolling', 'The king is dead! Long live the king'— all point towards the importance of 'don't stop, go on!' Life stops for no one; there should not be any stasis or stagnation: "Move—Move—Move in the forward direction towards the goal—

success is assured — we vouch for it", say psychologists and successful personalities.

Another act of moderation is the tactful and artful way to express your disagreement. When you want to contradict or disagree with somebody's opinion, action or manners, you must do it in a relaxed attitude or friendly good humour. You should not disagree by making noisy unpleasant scenes; or condescending statements.

When anything involves two entities there is bound to be difference of opinion, tastes, manners, etc. Views may be different. So when you cannot agree with others or when others can't agree with you disagreement ensues. This should be dealt with in a friendly manner.

You must concentrate on areas of agreement. A tolerant attitude must be exercised; any areas of disagreement must be sorted out by an amicable, friendly, pleasant approach. You should break the 'hostile barrier' and establish yourself as a welcome companion by adopting good humour and a congenial approach.

****

24

Success and Motivaion

All of us wish for the welfare and happiness of our brethren on this earth. *Sarvo Janah Sukino Bavantu*: let all the people live in happiness *Loka Samasta Sukino Bavantu* Let the entire world live happily. *San Mangalani Samati*—Let goodness, auspicious things prevail.*Vasudaiva Kutumbakam*: This entire world is one family. These are the teachings of Hindu religion. We are all in the same ship in the voyage of life. Let us wish good for all. The under motivated people complain about their poor opportunities. Everyone must provide unlimited opportunities for both under-motivated and well-motivated people. Opportunities must be in line with their eagerness for progress and willingness to earn the improvements.

Social movements (always upward) must be aimed at making everybody happy, satisfied, contented, pleased and self-sufficient.

'Mass equality' must be the goal. Everyone must think of sharing and not sparing. Everybody must be given chances, opportunities to serve, to seek pleasures and achieve his goal and success.

Successful people often talk about three important involvements:

1. Active involvement.

2. Non-involvement.
3. Selective involvement.

a. A person should involve himself in worthy causes which may need his and only his involvement. This advocates active involvement.

b. Youngsters, inexperienced and immature, rush off, heedless of consequences to get involved in every unworthy cause. This calls for non-involvement.

c. Involvement, which is concentrated in those worthy projects in which one can render a tangible personal service of consequence. This is the correct and the most appropriate sort of involvement—the selective involvement.

He should stay away from trivial, not-worth-a-penny causes. He should restrain himself from getting involved in such worthless causes which, apart from being useless, may even create unwanted consequences if he gets involved in it! Such causes are best left alone or left unnoticed.

Involvement in worthless causes can have adverse effects in the form of various blames on one — 'He took sides', 'He disagreed', 'He was the one who started it', 'He spoiled it' 'He was partial' etc. You must be cautious to avoid getting involved in such 'damage to reputation' causes.

Psychologists and successful men (out of their personal experience) offer an inspiring piece of advice which says:

"Never think that the job of succeeding is too big. Never give up when the going gets rough. Never think that the life goal is too far away. These are important to achieve success."

A person should assure himself that all his problems (if any) are insignificant and he has infinite power to tackle anything and everything on his way to achieving his goal. This self-assurance, self-confidence and proper perspective (in viewing your problems) guarantees success!

One of the important success strategies is to live in the

present and accept the fact that the past is gone. Past joys and past sorrows are past and the past is gone! Past joys and past sorrows are memories. You should never recincarnate them as present emotions. You must remember the past as past. You cannot relive the past. You cannot change the past. You can learn from the past mistakes though. Such learning should be

intellectual, not emotional. Close the door on the past and open the door on the present that is filled with opportunities and promising success!

Failure is one of the most effective methods used to succeed. Failure should not be feared and avoided. It should be accepted and used. Charles Catering, the great inventive genius of automobile engineering, said that 'learning to fail intelligently' is one of the keys to success. By failures you learn what will not work and therefore by elimination discover what will work! There are three classes of people:

1. Instant failures: Fail a few times, suffer ego damage, get discouraged and disheartened.
2. Permanent failures: Instant failures who quit become (Quick quitters) permanent failures.
3. Intelligent Failures or 'the successful' who know the difference between deliberate mistakes and honest mistakes.

Deliberate mistakes are sometimes done in spite of knowing or believing it to be wrong. It often leads to a feeling of guilt.

Honest mistakes are those which are the result of the valuable learning process of testing to find out what will not work so that by elimination you finally discover what will work. This ensures success. Thomas Edison devoted 10 years of continuing mistakes before he found the right way to make the nickel iron alkaline storage battery.

You should never resort to aggressive demonstrations, militant protests, picketing, boycotting, destructive disruption to solve problems. These are cheap strategies demanding dirty publicity. These are not to be used in achieving your goals. You should use wisdom. Success in family and personal relationships should be achieved by filling the 'understanding gap' with affection, joy, good humour, consideration, harmony, insight, compassion, support and thoughtful gestures.

When you talk with a person, you should say something which makes feel better. It may be an informal talk, a speech, a classroom lecture—it must always leave the listener, the audience with a satisfying experience. When the listener or audience feels better it improves personalities and attitudes. Success or failure is caused more by mental attitudes than by mental capacities. In the business or personal correspondence you should always write something which will make the recipient feel better.

When you make everyone feel better because of yourself, you start feeling better yourself! When somedody irritates or disagrees with you/ before jumping to immediate hostile conclusions give a thought. Assume that the person who is irritable or disagreeable may have some problems in his life. Give him the benefit of doubt. Treat him as someone who has been or is being hurt. You should treat such persons with kindness, understanding, tolerance and sympathy. It is important to know that the lives of many people may appear to be fine and attractive on the surface, but somewhere deep down they may have their problems, insecurities, inadequacies and defects. They may not like to exhibit it but its presence is causing them to be irritable or disagreeable.

Success strategies advocate you to control and change according to the demands of a situation. You should not just sit around affected by what happens. You should do something about what is happening. You should be managing or controlling the conditions to meet a change. You should act instantly to change a condition when it demands it. There is no use being a mute spectator, merely existing, changing nothing. You should not let your life be dominated or controlled by others.

You can have whatever you want to have!

You can be whatever you want to be!

You can do whatever you want to do!

For all this you have to raise to the occasion. You should not permit situations/conditions to have control over you. A man has this infiinite power capacity, alertness and capability to change anything. The need is the will do it. If he gets it he can work wonders!

There is an urgent need for soul searching. Anybody claiming to work for the underprivileged must ensure that what he is doing is for the real cause or for personal image building. You should never take up a cause for your image building. It should be always selfless. Motivation should be to serve a cause. Cheap publicity of self-proclaimed leaders of the masses must never be entertained. You should never use a noble cause for your personal interest and growth.

The successful people's biographies always advocate the four 'As' in a troublesome situation. They are:

1. Admit that the trouble is there.
2. Accept it if it is inevitable—as one of the changes of circumstance or luck.

3. Adjust to it. Successful personalities can adjust to a change, however unpleasant it is.
4. Act to improve the situation when a trouble is not inevitable.

You should decide whether to take it or leave it; consider it as a challenge. A person can take it. He can use his power, grit, determination—tackle it and feel the exhilaration of having fought it off. On the other hand, if the trouble has taken him to a dead end, a point of absolute, nothing can be done situation, then it will be best to leave it. There is no point in banging against a stone wall. For example, when a person is involved in an intolerably wrong career, he should leave it. In an incompatible marriage—where both the husband and wife have become strangers, with no love, understanding or respect for each other–it is better that they leave it. A person must use his power of judgement and discretion in deciding whether to take or leave a problem. In an intolerable situation it takes more courage and

The 4 A's to be followed in a troublesome situation.

Admit

Boss said that the heavy losses & the company may be shut down soon. That means I will lose my job.

Accept

I will need another job immediately. I have a family to support; loans have to be repaid.

Adjust

This kind of company shutdown, downsizing the staff, happens everywhere. I better complete by pending work.

Act

First let me check my savings; I have already applied for a job in 'xyz' company. Let me check it up; I will pass on my biodata to my friends. I must also see 'Job vacancy' columns.

intelligence to leave it and to more rewarding experiences instead of banging against the stone walls of that incorrigible situation claiming to be courageous.

Psychologists and people who have achieved success in their life say that one cannot be successful—lazily or indifferently or without intense thought and effort. Success is often a misunderstood concept. Many people believe that success is not easy for them as they have 'limitations', There is no condition or limitation that can prevent success if a person has the right thought and motivation. Always think of success as being easy. Never consider it a Herculean task. Never entertain thoughts suggesting 'limitations' that will stop success. Remember and practise the positive goal command, 'I will succeed', 'success is easy', mentally many many times and this can work wonders.

Be positive in your approach!

Sachin Tendulkar completed an unbelievable 10,000 runs in test cricket. He becomes the 5th cricket player in the world to complete 10,000 runs and go beyond it. In India, he is the 2nd player to achieve this mark after Sunil Gavaskar. On March 16, 2005, playing against Pakistan, Sachin made this record score.

This goes to prove that a positive approach with the right motivation can lead you to pinnacles of success.

Psychologists recommend solving problems one by one. The focus must be on one problem at a time. Problems must be disposed of one at a time. The rest of the problems, while solving one problem should not be considered as a burden but as a challenge. Responsibility, anxiety regarding a particular decision or solution to a problem must be kept at an optimum level—just enough to keep one going. Beyond that they should be dismissed as they can drastically decrease your working efficiency. When one problem has been solved you should move over to the next problem. This way of problem solving and decision making is methodical, logical and practical. You must bite only that much which you can chew at a time. If you bite more that a mouthful you will only choke. The same thing applies to problem solving. So keep your mind in calm equilibrium and remain cool.

****

25

Visualisation and Action

The word 'success 'means many things to many people but most people include money as one of the elements of success. This is natural and proper since money provides the means and the capability to do many necessary and worthwhile deeds and services which would be impossible without it. Financial advisors, economists, psychologists, success counsellors—experts who know about attracting and acquiring large sums of money—all agree that being 'money conscious' is a major essential. You can use coins and currency notes as concentration objects, think rich, handle money, repeating goal commands (related to money) mentally. Such methods make you money conscious. Since thoughts become one's future, such thoughts of money, riches, wealth take you towards you goal of becoming rich.

People persist in believing that things cannot be done! 'This cannot be done' attitude is a disease. One should be aware from newspapers and news channel bulletins that impossible things are being accomplished daily. The word 'impossible' carefully spelt, spells "I'm possible". Since the rewards for doing the impossible are instant wealth and fame you must not miss a chance in doing the impossible things. "Volunteer and be the first to do something which cannot be done if you expect the big reward."

No man is an island and he needs the cooperation, goodwill and help of people around him in his life. Here it will be interesting to learn about three kinds of people:

1. The will's — who oppose and obstruct everything.
2. The wont's — who oppose and obstruct everything.
3. The cant's — who fail at everything.

When you learn to classify the people as wills, won'ts and can'ts (which becomes easy with experience and practice) you will understand which group is the only group which can help you succeed. It is only the 'wills' who accomplish everything. Such people you should choose, contact and develop as sources, as associat and as friends. And how do you deal with the wont's and can'ts?

You should have the goodwill of the wont's (never ignore them or you should be charitable and encourage the can'ts'.

The people at the top of every business organisation have powerful friends who helped them get there and who can keep them there at the top! These friends are the 'wills' types. Modern business and modern living are all based on a complex structure of people, all dependent on one another, each contributing a part toward the whole or success of each other. You should develop a strong nexus with 'wills' type of people who contribute to your energy, talent, influence, power and success.

You should never insult or underestimate the talents of others. If you are successful, and have achieved a certain stature in society it doesn't mean others should be looked upon as useless failures. All the people need some psychological boosters. You should never discourage others. Every person needs some admiration, appreciation. Probably they have no such qualities, they have not done anything great — but there might be some (insignificant though) merit in them. You may have done something great and become an important person — remember that others also need to feel important. You can find and express something important about these supposedly unimportant people. This brings a sense of equality and unity among all people. Such attitude of a successful man makes his success more meaningful.

Psychologists and success counsellors stress the importance of imagination in making you what you want to become. Constantly visualising a mental picture of your ideal image or goal brings dramatic results. When a person clearly and intensely sees himself as if he has already become his ideal self — this imagination, 'vividly living' his future as he wants to be—will actually make him that in reality. Action (in this case becoming) must be consistent with constant thought. Thoughts—strong, intense, persistent—can translate a visualisation to reality.

Imagining, thinking and acting — as one wants to be in real life — can make anything come true. Just imagine again and again of being like a person (ideal). Over a period of time you become the kind of person you want to be! You are a super star of your own mental movie and in your imagination you become the kind of person you want to be. Then by intensely and constantly imagining yourself as the person you want to be, subconscious forces are set in motion, which create the actual fact.

Psychologists advice a step-by-step technique, first imagination, next thinking, finally acting, as you want to be. Thinking implies 'positive thinking.' Think success, visualise success and you will set in motion the power force of the realisable wish. When the mental picture or attitude is strongly held, it actually seems to control conditions and circumstances.

When you think as if you are successful, you rapidly acquire that all important, all powerful success attitude. Success or failure in boardrooms or courtrooms is caused more by mental attitudes than by mental capacities. Next comes the action. Action and feeling go together. By regulating the action, which is under the more direct control of the will, you can indirectly regulate the feeling. By acting as if you feel better, happy, confident, or courageous you actually cause yourself to feel the way you act.

Not only does action follow feeling, but also feeling follows action. If you act as if you are cheerful... you will feel cheerful. If you act as if you are confident... you will feel confident.

You can change or turn off undesirable and self-damaging feelings by acting. Suppose you are offended by your boss in the office, you begin to feel angry and resentful. You must change those self-damaging feelings by acting as if you are unperturbed by and tolerant of the rude boss — and instantly your feelings will change from resentment and anger to unperturbed tolerance.

Whenever there is some rude criticism or heated argument it is better that you have some well prepared responses. This will save ugly unpleasant scenes, hurt, heated exchanges and bitter feelings. Referred to as triggered automatic responses this refers to some well prepared, 'saves the ugly scene' and 'applies to every' expect rude criticism, and arguments.

These prepared automatic responses should be kept ready while expecting arguments, criticism (meant to discourages, demean and break one's spirit). When the argument or criticism actually comes it should trigger the well prepared, good natured, tolerant automatic response in the person. Such a response saves many a ugly scene and the critic gets the message.

Take, for example, a person whois well aware of his boss being caustic and sadistic when it comes to evaluating his work. He has had previous bitter experiences. Now he has to present his project file to the boss for evaluation. He wants to avoid ugly scenes and he wants to make it clear to the boss that he will not be affected by caustic, sadistic remarks. He can prepare a well rehearsed automatic response to be triggered on when his boss plays his usual game. See the following conversation.

The Boss: Your project work is as usual bad; not up to the mark; why don't you improve? Even a schoolboy can do a better job. I don't know how to correct you.

The boss's idea is to make the junior cry, break his zeal; demoralise him; shatter his self-confidence; and have sadistic pleasure.

The junior who expected this, triggers the automatic responses:

"You certainly have as much right to your opinion as I have to mine and you may very well be right." Or, you can say," "I understand how you feel and I understand why you feel as you do." Such triggered automatic responses are psychologically healthy and effective. They save heart breaks, exessive grief. You are mentally prepared and hence maintain your equipoise and dignity. Such responses point to a finality. No more nonsense, no more tears kind of conclusion. You avoid dirty heated exchanges, maintaining a polite, pleasant exchange to a 'meant to provoke'. tride remark. Such responses make you take control of the situation without agreeing with criticiser that he was right, without agreeing with the criticism without getting offended or provoked,and without getting to start 'a waste of time and energy, argument.

Whenever a photograph, object, memory of a sad event

comes to make you feel depressed or extreme grief you must have well prepared responses of love, nostalgia, etc. For example, at the death of a dear one, if you are prepared with happy moments shared with the departed, you can trigger this happy moment, relive it (in memories), cherish it and avoid depression, grief and sorrow.

Psychologists list five kinds of responses to a happening:

1. Over-response
2. Under-response
3. Delayed response
4. Non-response
5. Opposite response

A person responds in one of the five ways mentioned above to everything that happens to him—all day and every day. Which way he chooses to respond—and how successfully he responds—will greatly affect his success in life.

1. **Over-response:** Over-response with violence and anger makes one a loser when somebody says something insulting or infuriating. If the person receiving such caustic remarks over-responds by physically or verbally attacking the offender he ends up setting a chain reaction of future retaliation in the form of physical attacks, law suits, harm to family, business, career, etc.

   Any over-response in anger and violence triggers retaliation. Over-responses in fear, anxiety, panic etc., are never a solution. It greatly intensifies the problem. Over-response in the form of over-reacting is a form of 'ego inflation'. All these are harmful over-responses. Some over-respond to criticism by report. Criticism begets criticism in an escalating spiral and leads to pure uncontaminated resentment solving nothing.

Over-response solves nothing; it only increases and complicates matters and is damaging to one's personal growth and success. One should stay away from over-responses.

2. **Under response:** You should interpret under-response as a meeting with triumph and disaster and treating them as just the same. Under-response gives you a lot a control and with control comes power and leadership. It does not take life and its irritable people and annoying circumstances too seriously. It keeps you going smoothly through life with coolness and control.

3. **Delayed response.** A delayed response will give you time to first consider all possible alternatives before committing your-self. You should reach a decision after considering all the possible alternatives. This consideration should be done slowly but once the decision is made you should act rapidly. Delayed response need not be a time-wasting procedure. It should be a well planned and executed response. It is better that you do a right thing at the proper pace rather than doing wrong things quickly, on the pretext of doing something on time! Delayed reponse often rewards one with success.

4. **Non-response:** You should exercise your alternative of non-response very cautiously, very judiciously. You should not join every conflict or take sides in every controversial cause. You should not accept every task, shoulder every burden, assume every responsibility which may be thrust upon you. You need not worry about situations which need experts, opinion and skill. You should not involve yourself in every crisis which does not require your intervention. It is important that you should be well informed and interested in matters around you but involvement must be only in matters requiring your absolute presence. You should never do a thing just because you are expected to do it. You should

do a thing out of your own freedom of choice. This must be exercised with discretion. Things done under compulsion make you feel controlled, manipulated. Under all these circumstances you can opt for a non-response. Some things left alone are more beneficial than you getting involved. When you use your choice to remain non-responsive, you are able to deliberately and thoughtfully control your own acts. Non-response—the art of doing nothing—saves many a damaging situation. 'Let sleeping dogs lie, don't wake then' applies here. Why wake a sleeping dog and have it chase and bark at somebody? It may end up biting you. Such situations, where you are very well aware of the impending damaging consequences, if meddled with, need a non-response.

5. **Opposite response:** This is the art of doing the unexpected. Surprisingly it can be effectively implemented in many situations which are potentially unpleasant. If you respond to unpleasantness with the opposite response of pleasantness you become happy! If you respond to upleasantness with the expected responses of unpleasantness you end up in deep sorrow! Opposite responses can be a rewarding experience.

The inconvenciences and annoyances of life should be accepted not with an ill-tempered response or irritability, but with the opposite response of good humour. You should exercise the following opposite responses and enjoy the benefits.

Stimuli Response	Expected	Opposite response
i) Grievance	➔ Complaint	- Compliment
ii) Rudeness	➔ Hurt	- Sympathetic understanding

contd...

iii) Criticism	➔	Resentment		- Honest words of no appreciation for constructive advice.
iv) Dealing with adversary	➔	Enmity	➔	Do a favour with gracious friendliness.
v) Backbiting	➔	Anger	➔	One should respond to an unfavourable backbiting by making no favourable statements about the 'back biter'.

The above-mentioned opposite responses bring surprising, unexpected scenes and a person benefits to a great extent. Even rivals turn into friends, rudeness transforms into politeness, criticism becomes a nice advice, backbiting stops and turns into appreciation, when complaints are expressed as compliments. For example: instead of, "Your work is bad", if you say, "Your work is good but your calibre is much much more," there is a lot of moral boosting and support. The person who is receiving it becomes more responsible and his performance improves. Everything becomes positive instead of negative.

Your happiness and success in life will be greaty influenced by which response you choose and how effectively you use it.

Your should be diligent in your use of these responses. You must pick and choose, see the right situation, and use the right response. Intellect plays a major role here.

Psychologists and counsellors advocate two sensible pieces of advice:

1. You should always use more effective psychological methods than direct criticism when you expect certain positive results from others.
2. When others (who do not follow the above game plan) criticise a person you should respond by taking it as a positive advice. You should never entertain feelings of hurt to materialise. You should never take a criticism emotionally. You should strengthen and toughen your ego. Otherwise the 'ego damage' resulting from criticism can cause hurt. Criticism can be targeted against one for certain reasons.

1. The person (or the 'critic') who is criticising may try to release his pent-up frustrations and anger. Ignore and forget such criticism.
2. The critic may be on a mission to kill somebody's zeal, zest and enthusiasm. Beware of such criticism.

Sometimes the criticism may be a truth presented very harshly. You should take the truth part of the criticism as a helpful suggestion and discard the harsh, rude presentation. "Often the opinions and views of our enemies come nearer to the truth about us than do our opinions," said Rochefoucauld. Often the enemies are looking for your faults more intently than their own. You should ignore your enemy but never his criticism of you. The perfect way to deal with an enemy's criticism is:

1. First rid the criticism of all emotion — his and yours.
2. Criticism should be judged logically, impartially — solely on its merits—for it may reveal needed corrections which the friends hesitate to mention.
3. Criticism may be a good advice — without the sugar coating.

4. You can learn a lot from the criticism of an adversary or enemy if you do not let your judgement be distorted by your emotions of resentment/anger.
5. You should never refuse good advice because it comes in the form of criticism. Criticism sometimes is so valuable that you should voluntarily ask for it.
6. Remember the golden rule: most criticisms are helpful if you eliminate the emotions of both the giver and receiver. Criticism, like surgery, can remove the source of trouble and the cut will heal.

Psychologists always caution everyone to maintain a calm, cool, collected attitude to various things happening around them. Though easier said than done, this attitude can be achieved by practice and experience. You should never over-emotionalise, over dramatise or over-emphasise the passing events that constitute your life. Have an equal, unbiased, poised view on everything — triumph or disaster. Accepting failure and victory for what they are without any over-emphasis (which may discourage or make one over-confident) makes one stable and well controlled. One must accept the happenings of life with equanimity just as you accept the happenings of sunshine and rain, breeze and typhoon, full moon and no moon.

Certain general tips recommended by psychologists and success counsellors for a healthy mind, progress in life and to achieve success are:

1. One should never worry about what might happen in the future because anything can happen!
2. There is no point in worrying about the past, because the past is gone forever and cannot be changed.
3. You should never judge a person by his appearance. Appearances can be deceptive. Appearances of a person are never a limitation to his intellect, ability and talents.

4. It is better to avoid criticism (especially those negative, harming and sceptical ones) and friendly suggestions, sane advice and moral support statements.
5. Never advertise your weakneses or vices; they make you a weak prey to more bad habits and cheep practices.
6. You should never let an unhappy childhood experience affect your entire life.
7. You should never burden yourself with a multitude of tasks and responsibilities. Each day should be devoted to chores pertaining to that day only.
8. You should never waste your time thinking about someone you don't like. Why give unnecessary credit and importance to someone we dislike? One often hears the statement, 'The very thought of her gives me creeps'. Analysing this statement why think of her in the first place when 'creeps' is for sure to come? This time can be devoted in useful constructive actions.
9. You must always maintain a friendly attitude of conciliation and negotiate to achieve mutual resolutions.
10. You must associate your negative and undesirable habits or traits as being ridiculous, absolutely useless and must expel them from your system in an effective 'never again', assertive manner.

'Faith can move mountains', teaches the *Bible.* You should remove the various obstacles and opposing forces blocking your progress and life goal with faith and conviction. "Whatever a man can conceive and believe, man can achieve", is the law of life. With faith, conviction and efforts no obstacle or opposing force is formidable. This involves a two-step process:

First remove the fear, apprehension, fright, horror, panic, terror and dismay about an opposing force and obstacle blocking the life goal / progress. Next, come to the real obstacle/opposing force. Trust, certainty and determination can demolish any obstacle or opposing force.

****

26

Magnetism and Persistence

You must develop personal magnetism to achieve whatever you want. This personal magnetism is deliberately generated and intensified inside. This is called inner glow. This is then projected and radiated outside as an outer glow—which attracts others. This attraction becomes irresistible. Age or personal appearances are no limitations for one to develop personal magnetism. It is for everybody! Physical attractiveness differs in each individual depending on his physical appearance. Magnetic attractiveness is a skill that can be learned and used by everybody.

Your eyes are very important in radiating and projecting your personal magnetism. Eye magnetism is the name applied to this concept. Eye contact is an important aspect in any communication. You must look directly and deeply into the eyes of others. Eyes are your most effective way to communicate your personal magnetism. Only when the personal magnetism is communicated, attraction can happen. Next to this is eye contact. Eyes are the windows of your mind— you can make your mind communicate through your eyes and can also read the mind of others through their eyes. Then comes the eye language—actual expression in your eyes. This conveys your thoughts to the other person. Eye language is passing on messages through your eyes. The eye contact and the eye language pass on the 'eye message'.

This attracts people to a particular person as they sense his 'personal magnetism' through his eye. Psychologists recommend 'smile with the eyes' concept. You can smile with yous. When goodwill and good humour are relayed or transmitted throught the eye then you smile with your eyes! When the humorous twinkle lights up an eye, the eye begins to smile. This smile comes from the 'inner' core of a persons psyche. You must feel the goodwill, good humour sincerely before expressing it through your eyes. A genuine, sincere smile starts from within a person's being; not from a fake expression in his eyes. The rule is feel inside and smile through the eyes. The good-humoured, smiling eyes expression usually is sufficient and generally preferable for most occasions. Personal magnetism is radiated and expressed by smiling eyes. This attractive smile can do wonders to your personality and progress.

Next comes a magnetic voice! Voice projection is very important in bringing out one's personal magnetism. Thinking, feeling and directing one's voice to a person in front is an art. A person should project his voice by using the direction given by his thoughts. When the voice is projecting his thoughts, his eyes must also simultaneously speak. This synchronised use of eye expression and voice projection results in radiating a person's personal magnetism bring out his inner glow. This results in attraction influencing the people around and becoming an instant success!

Thinking and feeling completely controls voice projection and this must be synchronised or harmoniously matched with eye messages.

What is that inner glow which constitutes personal magnetism? The inner glow is a combination of physical, mental, emotional feelings. You must practise arousing intense feelings of alertness, excitement, exhilaration, elation, anticipation, confidence, emotional radiance. When these feelings are aroused

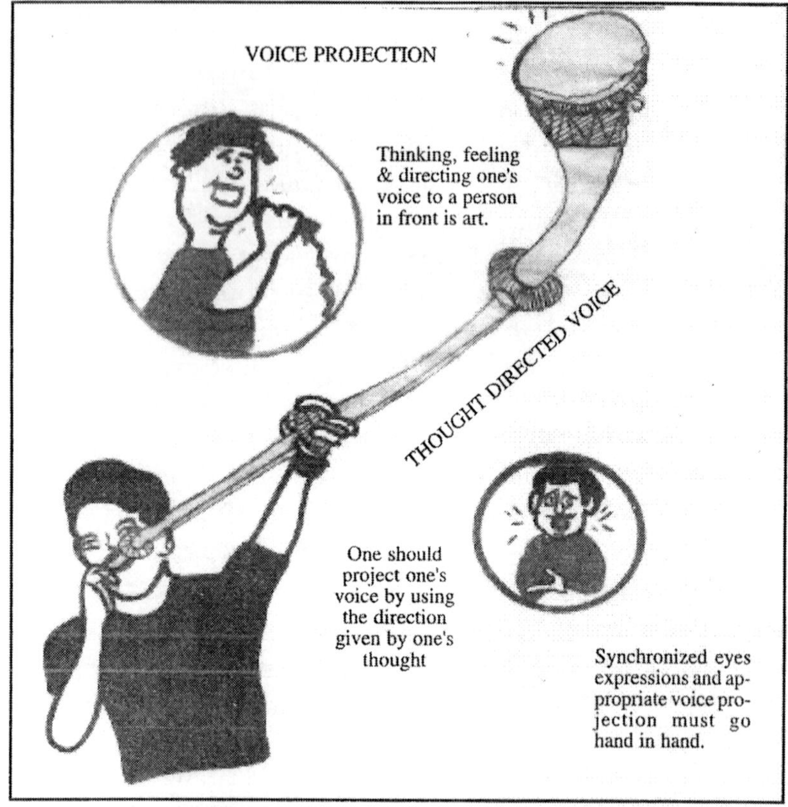

and intensified, this combined unit of aroused and intensified feelings constitute the 'inner glow'—this is projected or radiated. When this manifests by mental commands it becomes the outer glow. This outer glow becomes the personal magnetism attracting people around. The ultimate result is a successful, endearing personality.

Attracting people is an art. This personal magnetism makes one a source of fulfilment and people become attracted to the person to fulfil their subconscious needs. Every individual has needs. He likes to be accepted, approved, admired, appreciated, to feel important, to receive attention. All these compelling subconscious needs can become fulfilled by someone's personal magnetism. When a person fulfils the above needs of people around him, he becomes irresistibly attractive to them and his personal magnetism increases and intensifies too. The amazing potential of personal magnetism is to be explored for achieving one's goal and success.

William James, the Harvard philosopher and psychologist, said, "If you only care enough for the result, you will almost certainly attain it." That is, to become whatever you want to be in life, or want to achieve in life, you must care enough.

Only the power to care enough leads to achievement. If you only can care enough, you will try harder, and this leads to striving for more. These constant 'care enough' and 'try harder' efforts build a cascade. When these cascade reaches a point-where the cumulative effect of this 'care enough' 'try harder' efforts is at an optimum value, success, what started as a calm

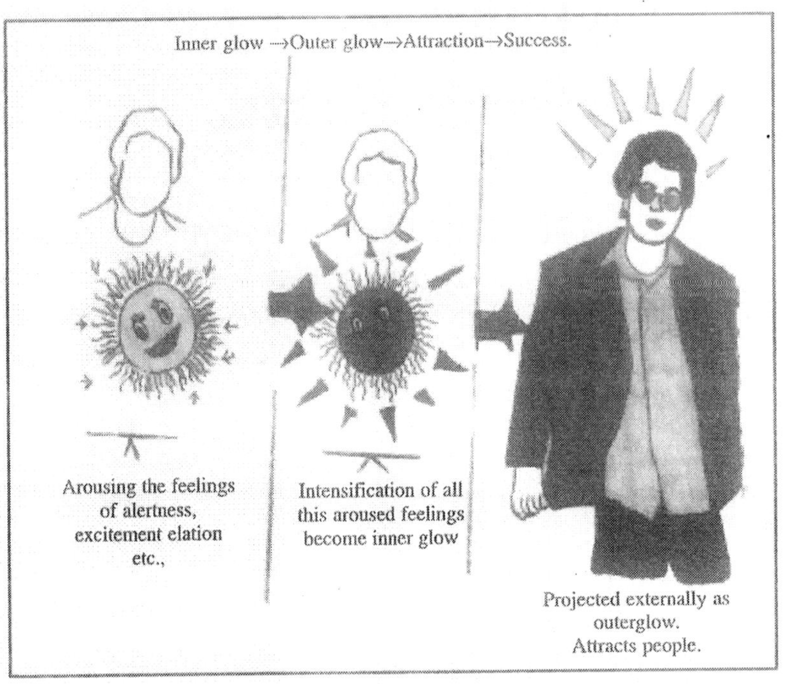

'care enough thought' picks up momentum with 'try harder efforts' and culminates into 'success' with dynamic speed.

Very few corporations, very few executives, very few employees, really care enough, so they do not try harder. Routine effort by most of the executives, employees, corporations is standard, usual procedure. They survive and often prosper only because their competitors do not caring enough and do not try harder either. By caring enough, trying harder and harder you can be exceptional, outstanding. Thus instant success is assured and you will be so much in demand that you get opportunities unlimited! The gains also becomes unlimited!

If a person has a worthy or compelling reason instead of selfish, self-centred ambitions his capability, capacity and power to achieve things become manifold. If he wants to become rich merely to loaf in idle luxury there will be no inspiration, no motivation or the power of a worthy, compelling reason. There will be only a plain selfish reason. Such plain selfish reasons or

desires driven by self-centered ambition's cannot contribute to the 'care enough', 'try harder' attitude. There will be no urgency or spirit to achieve the goal. In the case of 'becoming rich' the reason can be charity, money to help the underprivileged, to establish scholarships for meritorious students, grants for medical research. When money or riches are desired for such worthy causes, there is motivation and inspiration, all contributing to intense 'caring enough' and guided 'try harder' efforts. All these result in extra power, determination and grit. Soon the goal becomes clearer and nearer. A man attains wealth quickly and helps a worthy cause. Our subconscious mind translates only mental pictures into reality. Selfish desires are not strong enough and lack the impetus needed for such translations into reality.

"This life is short.
Vanities of the world are transient.
They alone live who live for others;
the rest are more dead than alive."
SWAMI VIVAKANANDA

A person must give up the 'lack of belief'. Most people just do not believe that they can do what, in fact, they can do with absolute certainty and relative ease—get whatever they want in life. Even if they develop some belief it is weak and uncertain. They end up quitting at their earliest. You should develop a strong enough belief to achieve your goal. This happens only by practice, effort and patience. Slowly and steadily the belief becomes strong enough to achieve the long cherished aim or goal. Psychologists prescribe a consistent, persistent, strong effort to develop belief is what one sets to achieve. Over a period of time this belief yields wonderful results. You should never weaken and lose your belief—this will be detrimental to your success!

Psychologists and counsellors list a few simple principle to achieve ones goal or success.

1. You should have a mental attitude of 'Persisting in progressing' towards your goal even when there are small setbacks.

2. Always consider failures as minor setbacks never credit them with titles of 'disasters' 'it's gone', 'it's finished' 'its over'.

3. You should make an intelligent use of your faults, failures and mistakes,"learning something from everything. Success or failure must be faced nonchalantly.

4. You should never settle for anything other than you goal. No second bests. No surrenders. If you aim for success and first place you should stick to your aims. You can accept anything better or supreme but nothing below your standard of achievements.

5. You should aim and work for superlatives, best things. You should never become complacent with mediocre, below average or substandard offers and positions.

6. Never remain undermotivated. If you make someone slog under inferior conditions the returns are few or nothing. You should become strongly motivated, put yourself in a commanding position and aim for the stars. You may not reach them but can chart your course by them!

7. You should remember the three DO's:

   a. Do the thing you have to do.

   b. Do it when it ought to be done.

   c. Do it whether you like it or not.

   You should acquire the necessary will, ability and motivation to make you do a thing which you have to do, at an appropriate time.

8. The fact is that whatever you want in life is not some impossible dream. It exists, you don't have to create it. You merely have to discover it because it exists now—waiting for you to discover and possess it. You need to tune in your subconscious mind and you are bound to achieve your desired goal.
9. You should devote some sizable part of your time in physical and mental exercises. Whatever be the age you should never give up these healthy practices. Nobody is old and incapable. 'Think young' and this can do wonders.

Think young leads to the 'live young' concept. You should

never give up your interests, hobbies or personal likings because of increasing age. You must prepare to live by expanding your interests, ideas and activities instead of preparing to die by limiting yourself to mere 'existence' or by giving up interests, ideas and inspiring thoughts. The calendar does not determine your health or the length of your life or your enthusiasm for living it. The young should motivate the old and vice versa by their thoughts, action, words.

10. When something happens in the mind, it also happens in the body. This is called psycho-physical parallelism. We are all aware of mental conditions in us, the psychosomatic disorders. Our thoughts create corresponding physical changes. You must control your subconscious by your constant, intense and positive thoughts—and this will bring about a healthy body, a healthy mind and a bright future!

****

Part-V

MOTIVATING CONCEPTS

27

Inspiring Mords of Famous Men

Get Motivated

A journey of a thousand miles must begin with a single step.

Lao Tzu

"Time is Money"

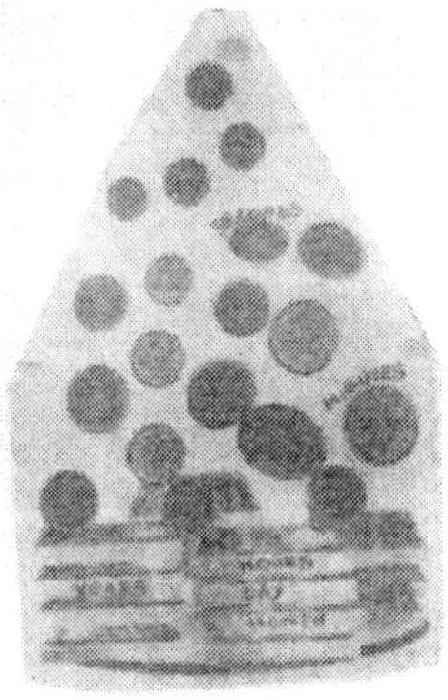

Good is not good where better is expected.

Thomas Fuller

We are not here to play, to dream, to drift—we have hard work to do and load to lift, shun not the struggle. Face it—it's God's gift.

Goethe

The shortest way to do anything is to do only one thing at once.

Samuel Smiles

Life is a great surprise. I do not see why death should not be an even greater one.

Vladimir Nabakov

To know how to say what other people only think, is what makes men, poets and sages;
and to dare to say what others only dare to think, makes men martyrs or reformers.

Elizabeth Rundle Charles

Man wanders over the restless sea,
The flowing water and the sight of the sky,
And forgets that of all wonders,
Man himself is the most wonderful,

St. Augustine

Nothing succeeds like the appearance of success.

Christopher Laseh

A scene of duty is useful in work, but offensive in personal relations. People want to be liked, not to be endured with patient resignation.

Bertrand Russell

The possibility that we may fail in the struggle ought not to deter us from the support of a cause we believe to be just.

Abraham Lincoln

Remember that time is money

Benjamin Franklin

Trust no future,
however so pleasant!
Let the dead past bury its dead!
Act, act in the living present!
Heart within and God overhead!

Longfellow

Life is mostly froth and bubble.
Two things stand like stone—
Kindness in another's trouble,
courage in your own.

A.L. Gordon

Perfect freedom is reserved for the man who lives by his own work, and in that work does what he wants to do.

G. R. Collingwood

Life shrinks or expands in proportion to one's courage.

Anais Nin

There is no such thing as can't, only won't. If you are qualified all it takes is a burning desire to accomplish, to make a change. Go forward, go backward. Whatever it takes! But you can't blame other people or society in general. It all comes from your mind. When we do the impossible we realise we are special people.

Jan Ashford

Grab a chance and
you won't be sorry
for a might have been.

Arthur Rensome

We have no more right to consume happiness without producing it than to consume wealth without producing it.

George Bernard Shaw

Of time, nothing profits more than self-esteem, grounded on just and right well managed.

John Milton

make
war than to
make
peace. *Georges Clemenceau*

It is easier to
If A is success in life, then
A equals x plus y plus z.
Work is x; y is play;
and z is keeping your
mouth shut.
– *Albert Einstein*

Three passions, simple but
overwhelmingly
strong, have governed my
life:
The longing for love, the
search for knowledge and
unbearable pity for the
suffering mankind.
—*Bertrand Russell*

Labour is the poor man's
pride
Success by toil alone is
won.
King's glory in
possessions wide,
we glory in our work well
done.
Schiller

The chief function of a city
is to convert power into
form, energy into culture,
dead matter into the living
symbols of art, biological
reproduction into social
creativity.
Lewis Mumford

The depth and strength of a human character are defined by its moral reserves. People reveal themselves completely only when they are thrown out of the customary conditions of their life, for only then do they have to fall back on their reserves.

Leon Trotsky

There is a difference between the things we want and our basic needs. If we will ask not for things, but for wisdom to understand what is right for us, then we shall have everything that we need and we shall learn those were the things we really wanted all the time.

Dr. Robert Anthony

IF

By Rudyard Kipling

If you can keep your head when all about you are losing theirs and blaming it on you.

If you can trust yourself when all men doubt you but make allowance for their doubting too;

If you can wait and not be tired by waiting, or being lied about, don't deal in lies, or being hated, don't give way to hating, and yet don't look too good, nor talk too wise;

If you can make one heap of all your winnings and risk it on one turn of pitch-and-toss, and lose and start again at your beginnings and never breathe a word about your loss;

If you can force your heart and nerve and sinew to serve your turn long after they are gone, and so hold on when there is nothing in you except the will which says to them: "Hold on!"

If you can talk with crowds and keep your virtue, or walk with kings—nor lose the common touch;

If neither foes nor loving friends can hurt you;

If all men count with you, but none too much,

If you can fill the unforgiving minute with sixty seconds worth of distance run;

Yours is the earth and everything that's on it; and — which is more — you'll be a man, my son!

This poem by Rudyard Kipling is a piece of real motivation to all of us. If only we can follow even 1 per cent of what is listed in the poem, we can go to great heights!

I do not know how I appear to the world, but to myself I seem to have been only a boy playing on the seashore and diverting myself now and then finding a smoothed pebble or a prettier shell than ordinary, whilst the great ocean of truth lay all undiscovered before me.

Isaac Newton

****

28

Motivating Expressions

Get Motivated

Look at these pictures. Each has a motivating message.

'Be many things but never ordinary' emphasizes the spirit of this surfer.

Look at these small children so very eager to learn computers.

'Update your knowledge and get going'

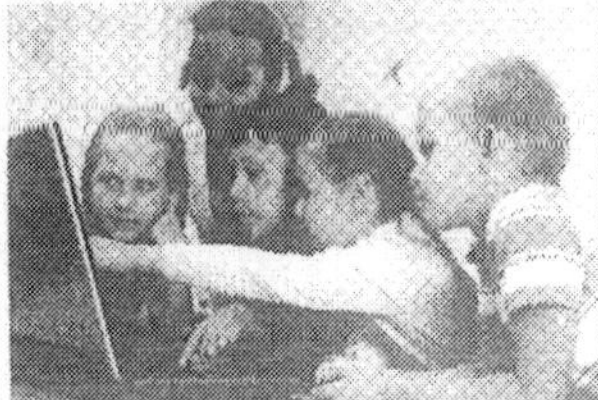

The snile on this blind boy's face is a message for all of us who are forever complaining about deficiencies and miss out on our abundance

Look at these tribal women making incense sticks. Self- sufficiency, importance of economic independence 'and hard work—these are the messages of this picture.

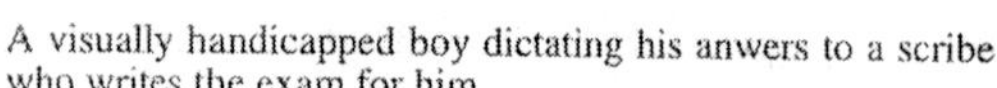

A visually handicapped boy dictating his anwers to a scribe who writes the exam for him.

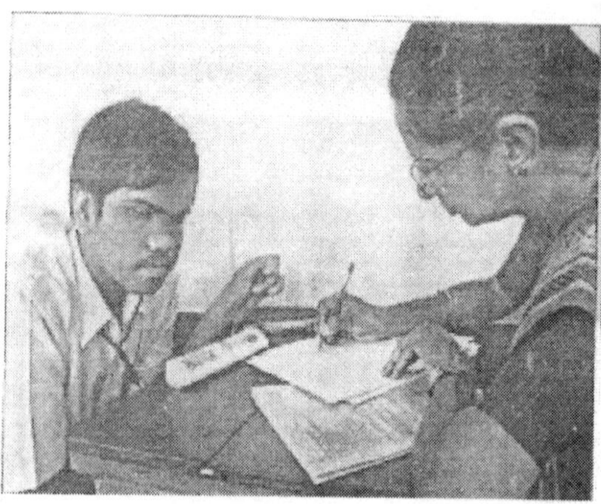

The boy is an example of determination and grit.
The scribe is an example of selfless attitude and has risen in her status from being self-centred to being altruistic.

'Whatever be your field of excellence, aim for the sky' motivates this picture

Enjoy life
to its fullest!
self-help
Planning
Looking
WATCH
EXPAND your horizon!
LEAD
positive
Dream
THE BEST
better
growth and prosperity.
Haste makes waste
Find yourself
passion
Climbing right ladders
New
Arrival
Light
UPDATE

29

Words That Matter

What do the following 20 words mean to you?

1. Enjoy life to its fullest.
   * Get pleasure from every aspect of life.
   * Delight in, love, relish.
   * Have the use or benefit of everything that life has to offer.

2. Self-help
   * Be independent, self-sufficient.
   * Do not be dependent on or controlled by another person or thing.
   * Financial independence.
   * Self-reliant.

3. Planning, looking

   Plan your present, future. Look for inspiration. Look for opportunities. Look for role models and then plan how you can become a role model.

4. Watch
   * Watch your success rate.

	* Watch your progress.
	* Watch your adversaries.
	* Watch out and be on guard.
5. Lead	* Lead your team.
	* Influence your team into action, success.
	* Be in first place or ahead.
	* Develop leadership qualities.
6. Expand your horizon	* Become more genial.
	* Enhance your importance: become more important, do more important things
	* Spread your outlook, don't be narrow minded.
	* Broaden your knowledge, interests, scope.
	* Realise your potential. Explore it.
7. Positive	* Be definite in your thoughts, words, action.
	* Be certain in your decisions.
	* Be clear in your plans, ideas.
	* Get convinced in your success.
	* Be confident, sure, satisfied.
	* Be productive, constructive, favourable.
8. Dream	* Dream up, imagine, invent, create, conceive.
	* Develop aspirations, hopes,

	ambitions, ideals.
	* Wish for success, achievement.
	* Fantasise.'success'; make it happen.
9. The Best	* Be best in everything you do.
	* Excel.
	* Be of the 'finest' in thoughts, words, action.
	* Be first class in all your endeavours.
	* Aim for the top.
	* Be the most useful, excellent in your field.
10. Growth and Prosperity	* Develop your field of excellence of better ideas, plans.
	* Broaden your view, thoughts.
	* Progress.
	* Be successful.
	* Flourish.
	* Financially be successful.
11. Better and Best	* For those striving to be the 'best', being 'better' serves as a stepping stone.
	* For the winners it is "never settle for anything better go for the best"
	* Try, Try, Try again, put in more efforts; do well.

* Get the better of your rivals.
* Do well for the better part of your life.

12. Keep Discovering

Be innovative in your thoughts, actions.

* Learn.
* Introduce something new, be novel.
* Develop fresh concepts, ideas.
* Be different.
* Welcome new concepts, thoughts,
* Gain knowledge and skills continuously.
* Pick up modern ideas.
* Notice-perceive-realise new concepts.

13. Haste makes Waste

* Don't be impulsive in decisions.
* Don't be headless.
* Don't be careless and reckless.
* Think and then proceed.
* Well planned calm actions yield profits.
* Adequate results are not achieved if something is done in haste.

14. Find Yourself

* Discover your potentials.
* Discover your plus and minus points.

* Improve your personality.
* Unearth your talents.
* Mask your shortcomings.
* Make a 'self-study' work out on your attributes, augment the positive points; improve the average points; delete the negative points.

15. Passion

* Develop a passion for your work.
* Be passionate about your work and results.
* Have ardent interest in anything and everything connected with your success, achievements.
* Have intense interest in your field of excellence.

16. Climbing Right Ladders

* Be in the right place at the right time.
* Aim for the top position in your field of excellence and work for it.
* To grow in your field of excellence you must work, and do the appropriate tasks.
* Climb the right ladders. In essence it means growth in the right direction, ascending right

steps towards one's goal and success.

* Go up in search of the peak (in one's field).
* Ladder refers to using right tactics.
* Promotion, increment.

17. New
* Be modern in outlook and actions.
* Be fresh, novel.
* Develop innovative, different ideas.
* Learn all the recent developments.
* Be trendy.

18. Arrival
* Make a grand appearance wherever you go and whatever you do.
* Entrance(your boss, your unions).
* Make a long lasting impression on everybody's mind.
* Your appearance must signify arrival of new ideas: great actions and credibility.

19. Light
* Success.
* Attainment of one's aims, wealth, fame.
* Victory, triumph, profit.

GROWT

'Climbing right ladders' mean 'Growth'→Grow in the right direction
→Make right efforts to promote yourself
→Be in the right place at the right time to attain top position.

* Cheerful, sunny, happy, merry.
* In good spirits.
* Brighten up.
* Promising, favourable.

  optimistic, hopeful.

20. Update

* Know to update your knowledge.
* Be modern, know of recent developments.
* Look for new opportunities in

  the recent field of development.
* Observe, assimilate and absorb all that is currently in vogue, fresh, modern and new.
* Keep abreast of every new event, happening.

30

Motivating Examples 'Vitamin - M'

To achieve success in any business venture a person needs vitamin M. The M stands for

1. Money
2. Machine
3. Manpower
4. Method
5. Market
6. Material
7. Motivation

The business can be managed with a short supply of the first six ingredicnts. But the seventh ingredient is needed always in excess.

The Fantastic '38'

Better late than never goes the saying. But late ventures can be a big success. An interesting statistics shows that 38 is the age for creating excellence and world record.

1. Neil Armstrong stepped on the moon at the age of 38.
2. German engineer Voltis discovered diesel oil at the age of 38.

3. Ellis who wrote the famous book titled *Psychology of Sex*, wrote when he was 38 years old.
4. Herpp'rlon discovered polaroid camera when he was 38.
5. Charles Devins, a scientist, discovered laser rays when he was 38.
6. Joseph Lister discovered antibiotics when he was 38.
7. Mary Fallopian discovered at the age of 38 the fact that the fertilized ovum travels to the uterus via ovarian tube,

Age 38 seems to be the age for achievements!

Age no Bar for Achievements

1. Youngest Indian to score a century in test cricket: Sachin Tendulkar.
2. Oldest person to assume the office of the prime minister of India: Morarji Desai.
3. The king of pop, Michael Jackson, was a founder member of the Jackson five at the age of 4.
4. Atal Bihari Vajpayee, in spite of being a septagenerian, was appointed prime minister of India thrice.
5. Akbar, the great Mughal king, was only 14 years old when he first became king.

Management Miracle of 20th Century

Forbes tallied his worth at $ 1.3 billion, making him the richest Hispanic in the USA. When he died of lung cancer in October 1997, he was instantly hailed as the management miracle of this century. Born and raised in Cuba, he embodied the American dream; immigrant, tireless and loyal employee, the boss and the paragon of Capitalism. He never worked for any other company. Can you recognise the person we are talking about?

Coca Cola's remarkable Roberto Goizuetta who is credited with turning a conservative company into a global giant.

Hard Work, Efforts Pay!

1. Lost his job in 1832.
2. Defeated for the legislature in 1832.
3. Suffered a setback in business in 1833.
4. Defeated for the speaker of Illinois state legislature in 1838.
5. Defeated for the vicepresidentship in 1856.

   With all these setbacks this man emerged as a person known for tremendous political achievements: *Abraham Lincoln*

Come What May, Talent Can Be Suppressed

1. Before he got the Nobel Prize, Rabindranath Tagore's poem were often termed 'faulty'. They were pointed out to be full of errors. His poems were printed in "Spot and correct the errors " columns of magazines. However, once he got the Nobel Prize they were withdrawn.
2. Before the William Sisters (Serena and Venus), only one Black had got Wimbledon Title. In woman's title ALTHIA GIBSON got the title in 1957 and 1958. In 1990 Jeena Garison came up to the final round. And in 2000 Venus Williams won the title. After 1958, 42 years later, a Black got the title again. This is true talent, hard work and motivation!

They All Made It Big!

1. American minister Jimmy Carter was a salesman.
2. The ex-Soviet President and Nobel Prize winner Michail Gorbachev was an operator in a tractor station in a small village of Russia, working for 12 hours a day.

3. American President George Bush (Senior) was an equipment checker in an American establishment.
4. Ex-British Prime Minister John Major could not even pass a bus conductor interview. He became a building contractor supplying cement, bricks. But this failed and he was penniless for long months!

5. Hollywood actress Sophia Lauren was a cartoon artist.
6. Hollywood actor Sylvester Staleone was a beauty salon assistant; In his 16 years' school life he was dismissed from 14 schools.
7. Cricket player Vivian Richard was a motor mechanic.

This Is Called Excellence

1. Scientist Sir C.V. Raman got both Nobel Prize and Bharat Ratna.
2. Lata Mangeshkar got both Dada Saheb Phalke Award (1989) and Bharat Ratna.
3. Satyajit Ray got both Dada Saheb Phalke Award and Bharat Ratna.
4. J.R.D. Tata and M.S. Subbalakshmi were awarded the Bharat Ratna.

What a Life! – Inspirimg and Motivating

1. Thomas Alva Edison discovered 1,300 things. For 1,093 things he got the copyrights from the American government.

   He had made 3,500 notebooks—containing the notes,

procedures and various processes involved in his discoveries and inventions.

2. He was very hard working. To make a tungsten filament he repeated experiments 1,200 times!
3. To make a perfect bulb Edison made 40,000 pages of notes in 200 notebooks under the heading 'light'.
4. He failed in his efforts many times but never gave up.
5. The magazine *Times* (Issue dated 31.10.1999) describes Edison as a man whose discoveries/inventions modernised the world and remodelled the future.

The Japanese don't have the word 'REST' in their vocabulary. There is not even an equivalent to this word. Probably this accounts for their success!

Prove Your Critics Wrong

1. Olympics Year 1936: Jessie Owens won four gold medals in Athletics and disproved Adolf Hitler's claim that 'Blacks can never defeat the Whites in sports,
2. Winston Churchill— In the Second World War Hitler's ideas were devastated by Churchill and, England won the war. Churchill was the world's only prime minister to get a Nobel Prize for literature. He was a very dull student in his school days, always awarded the last rank, failed in his 6th standard. He always believed that one can win and achieve beyond academics by working hard. He worked very hard and became the Prime Minister of England one fine day!

Observation Leads To Success

Doctor Rene Theophile Laennec one day saw some children scratching one end of a long wooden beam with a pin and listened to the sound transmitted through the beam at the other end. That gave him an idea. He carved a wooden cylinder one foot long and made perforations at one end and fixed an earpiece at the other end. The stethoscope. The year was 1816. He put the perforated end of the tube to a patient's chest and listened to the noises made by the heart and lungs. He compared the noises made by different patients suffering from different illnesses and at different times. In 1819, he published the findings and the stethoscope began to be used for diagnosing diseases. The modern stethoscope facilitates listening by both ears.

Nothing Is Impossible!

Do you know that the Oscar Award (so famous and so coveted) was designed by Cedric Gibbons within five minutes on a tablecloth of the Bilimore Hotel.

If there is talent, determination, motivation and skill nothing is impossible.

Winner ... Winner... All the Way!

Pete Sampras won his first slam in Flushing Meadows at the age of 19 in 1990. His last was in 2000. He has 64 single titles and this includes a record 14 at grand slams.

His achievements reflect his attitude to be the 'best' in his field. His grit, determination and hard work won him all the titles!

A Humble Start But Great Stop.

Do you know the master of crime stories, Alfred Hitchcock? He was the son of a poultry dealer, good at drawing and designing captions for silent films. He later directed movies in Britain before moving over to Hollywood. He often caught his audiences out with nasty surprises. He was knighted shortly before his death in 1980.

Looking at his life one sees a very humble start but his hard work, talent, efforts took him to great heights. Hailed as the king of suspense thrillers he stopped only by achieving knighthood!

Thoughts Can Create Wonders

Rolls was a car dealer. Royce was an iron merchant. They had never met before. Rolls always dreamt of designing a high-class car. Royce wanted to manufacture a luxury car. Both

Rolls Royce

were making efforts on their own way. Once they met by chance. Royce discussed his idea with Rolls. He was overjoyed. Royce explained that he wanted to manufacture a very nice, easy and comfortable-to-travel luxury car. Rolls said that he was interested in the idea and he would design a first class car. Both were not bothered about the cost and aimed at designing and making a car of first class nature, unique and sleek. They decided to name the car after their names, symbolising the oneness in their thought and idea. Thus came the glossy Rolls Royce car!

Make a Difference

1. Henry Ford — Discovered motor car.

   Established an automobile industry . Became a millionaire!

2. German Composer Beethoven, in spite of his handicaps, made fantastic compositons. His compositions even included events such as impact of French Revolution

3. Voltas discovered the electric batteries. The unit volt got named after him!

4. Walt disney got the highest number of (17 of them) Oscar Awards for his films.

   Achievements, inspiration, faith and motivation, are four words often misunderstood. These words should be properly interpreted and followed.

1. **Achievement:** Need not be always in terms of name, fame and money, it can be an outstanding accomplishment with a totally different message.

2. **Inspiration:** Need not always come from successful people and their attitude sometimes a very 'different' concept or person inspires, stimulates and arouses our dormant potential.

3. **Faith:** We look for faith in all the wrong things — cults, mantras chanted by spurious gurus, talismans and rings/ chains.

   Our Hindu *Puranas* have tremendous episodes to define what true faith is.

4. **Motivation:** Should come not from data but by the message behind it.

Achievements

Achievements and accomplishments can happen beyond boardrooms and court rooms. See the following pictures.

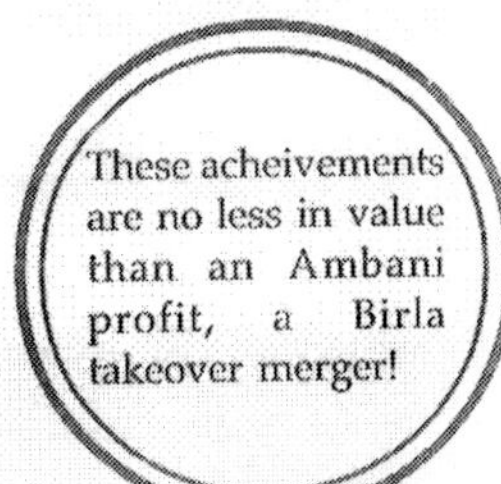

Upendra Kumar, a youth from Motihari, Bihar writes his school final exams with his feet.

(Note: His hands are invalid, not his will power.

There was a racing event conducted for the handicapped in Amritsar, Punjab recently. Look at the way this participant joins the race with the help of a chair.

Inspiration Swirling on a Bed of Nails

Kuala Lumpur, May 31. An instructor of Indian traditional dance swirled and swayed on a bed of nails for more than 30 minutes in Malaysia — leaving her with slightly bloodied feet and claims to a record.

S.Mathevi, (see picture on next page) in bare feet and traditional Indian costume, performed Bharatanatayam on a floor of about 10,000 nails in the central city of Ipoh to help raise awareness of the non-nail version of the art form.

She also claimed to have set a record for the length of time spent dancing on a bed of nails, and hoped her feat over the weekend would be included in the Malaysian

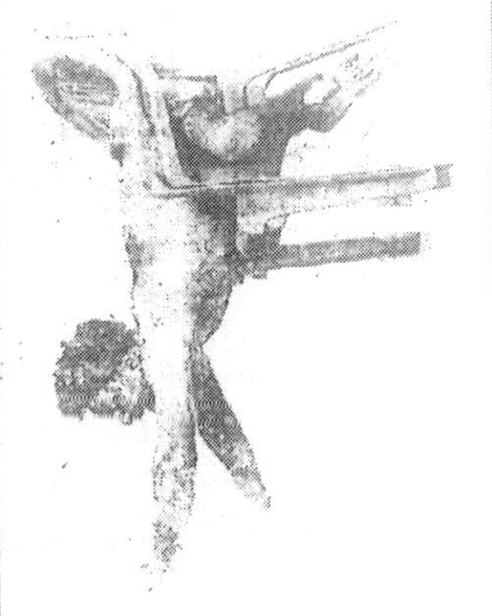

There was a racing even't conducted for the handicapped (?) in Amritsar, Punjab recently. Look at the way.
This participant joins the race with the help of a chair.
(Note: How can he be called handicapped when his spirits and novale are so perfect?

Book of Records and featured on the U.S. television show 'Ripley's Believe it Or Not.

'Faith Can move Mountains' Says the *Bible*

Our Hindu *Puranas* have plenty of stories bearing testimony to this principle. The prince Prahlada had immense faith in Lord Vishnu. When Prahlada's cruel father, the demon king Hiranyakashipu, tried to kill him by making the cruel snakes Vasuki and Dakshan crawl over him and inject their poison (venom) Prahlada came out unscathed by his faith. The venom turned into nectar and protected him! Next, Hiranyakashipu planned to kill Prahlada by making huge elephants stamp over him. Prahlada came out of this too unscathed! His faith in Lord Vishnu crushed the tusks of elephants when they hit him on his chest. Remember this story. Faith in self, God and in one's principles, having firm conviction, can create wonders!

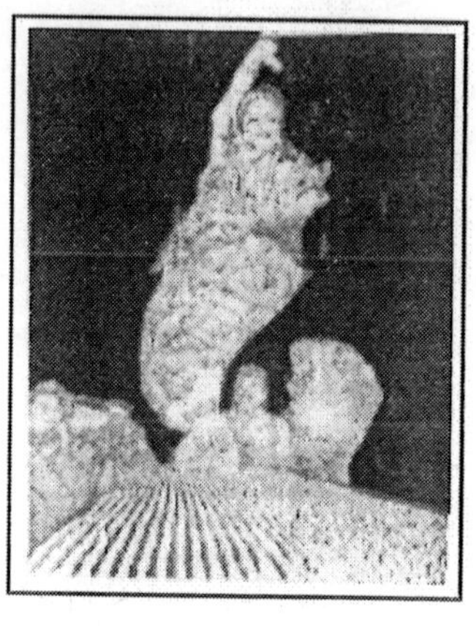

Motivation

The Economic Times recently published a list of India's 25 richest persons. Out of the 25 we will just look at the financial profile of the following six men.

1. Lakshmi N Mittal.India's No.1 richest man.

   His assets are worth 1,10,000 crores.

   His business includes steel manufacture.

2. Asim Premji (WIPRO).

   He was in the No.1 slot of Indian richies for more than 10 years.

   He specialises in software, oils, soaps etc.

His assets are worth Rs.40,920 crores.

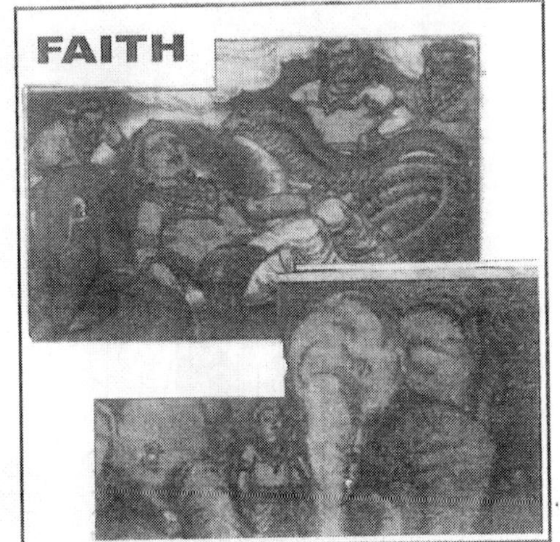

3. Mukesh and Anil Ambani.

   Owner:

   Reliance Group of Companies.

   Deal with petrol -eum, textiles, etc . Assets:

   Rs.30,800 crores.

4. Kumar Birla.

   Aditya Birla Group of Companies.

   Deal with aluminium, textiles, metal, communication, etc.

   Assets worth Rs.16,280 crores

5. Sunil Bharti Mittal.

   New generation 'richie'.

   'Bharti Group.

   Telecommunications

   Assets Rs.14,520 crores.

6. Shiv Nadar

   HCL Group.

   Assets worth Rs.10,120 crores.

Here the financial figures and data are not the motivating factors. The hard work, sweat, determination, efforts and tenacity which have gone into making such assets and success are the motivating factors. For every cause there is effect. Get

Lakshmi N. Mittal Azim Premji Ambani Brothers

Kumar M.Birla Sunil Mittal Shiv Nadar

Our assets of hardwork, grit & determination are more valueable than our financial assets.

motivated by the cause and the effect will follow. Never get motivated by the effects!

Dheeru Bhai Ambani painstakingly established the Reliance. Group of companies. In the year 1981 Mukesh Ambani came into the establishment. Within the next two years Anil Ambani also took charge of the management. The rest is history. The two brothers very skilfully, with sweat and toil, marched forth on the footsteps of their father and diversified the Relianc Group into many different specialities. The father sowed the seed, the sons nurtured, and grew the Reliance into a full-fledged tree with innumerable branches. Their foray has been into every possible field. The motivation message is painstaking hard-work, intelligent moves, business acumen, efforts put in the right ventures in the right measures at right times.

Kumaramangalam Birla took charge of the Birla Group when he was just 28 years old. He took the group in the path of progress, development and growth. The motivation message should be his progressive ideas, zeal and zest to excel, energy, vigour and vitality and, last but not least,the sweat and toil.

Sunil Bharti Mittal is regarded as a new generation richie.

In a very short span of time he has secured a top position in the Indian telecommunication industry. The motivation message should not be the Rs.14,520 crores but the efforts, strenuous attempts, long working hours putting the personal interests at the back and working towards the countrys and the company's interests.

Here it will be interesting to know about Lakshmi N. Mittal. He is the number one Indian rich guy that everybody knows but he is ranked number three among the world's richest people list. After Bill Gates and Waren comes Lakshmi N. Mittal. His assets worth Rs.1,10,000 crores should motivate one; the extreme levels of hard work, business skills, sharp decisions, right use of the opportunities — all these have earned him the much deserved success. These qualities should motivate each person aspiring and looking for ways to success.

Infosys: Profits Soar

Bangalore: Riding on the outsourcing boom, software major Infosys Technologies reported a net profit of Rs.1,89,167 crores for the year ended March 31, 2005, a leap of 52.11 per cent turnover of Rs.1,243.63 crores posted in the previous year.

The Nasdaq listed the company posted full year revenues of Rs.7,129.65 crore, an increase of 46.91 per cent over Rs. 4,852.95 crores earned in 2003-4, an Infosys statement said here. The net profit for 2004-05 includes Rs.45.19 crores from the sale of stake in the U.S. based Yantra Corporation.

Recently this piece of news appeared in all the newspapers. The data and figures here are not impressive but the hard work, planning, the humble start to rapid growth journey, the working momentum, team work and spirit — all these which have produced these profits are inspiring and motivating beyond words! These hidden messages must be the motivating factor for all the people looking for success in their lives. The message is loud and clear: the path to excellence is long and tiresome. There are no shortcuts for success and achievements!

Microsoft's New Initiative In India

Incubation of fresh ideas and technology innovation Microsoft, which started its Indian operations with 20 people in 1998 now has its own 2.6 lakh sq. ft. development centre at Hyderabad with 500 people, with the second phase in progress over a 28-acre site. The IDC here has filed 40 patents last year and expects to file 70 this year.

We are all aware of Bill Gates, his astounding and meteoric climb from being a nobody to being the be-all and end-all'. The above piece of news does not motivate by its figures, but by the 'go ahead' 'win it' spirit of Microsoft and the brain behind it—Bill Gates. When any person gets true motivation (not from the data/figures) but from the 'sweat and toil' creating those figures he is bound to succeed. Nothing can stop him! Get motivated by the overpowering', nature of the winners, not by their company turnovers!

****

Bibliography

M.R. Kopmeyer, *Here's Help!*

Smt. Jaya Row, *Bhagavad Gita* lectures.

Swami Vivekananda, *Personality Development.*

Newspaper articles and journals.

Several articles, excerpts from Tamil weeklies, books, etc.

Certain movies, their contents.

Opinions and views of experts.

Psychological journals.

Su-ki-Sivam's inspiring articles.